Christian Assemblies for Primary Schools

Also by Sharon Swain and published by SPCK:

The Sermon Slot: Ideas for All-Age Worship Year 1 (1992)
The Sermon Slot: Ideas for All-Age Worship Year 2 (1993)
More Christian Assemblies for Primary Schools (1998)

SHARON SWAIN

Christian Assemblies for Primary Schools

Linking worship to National Curriculum
class activities

First published in Great Britain 1995
Society for Promoting Christian Knowledge
Holy Trinity Church
Marylebone Road
London NW1 4DU

Bible readings are from the *Good News Bible (Today's English Version)*,
published by Bible Societies/HarperCollins, © American Bible Society,
New York 1966, 1971, 1976.

British Library Cataloguing-in-Publication Data

A catalogue record for this book is available from the British Library

ISBN 0–281–04792–8

Typeset by Wilmaset Ltd., Birkenhead, Wirral
Printed in Great Britain by The Cromwell Press, Trowbridge, Wiltshire

Contents

Introduction

This book offers primary school teachers bright, user-friendly ideas to conduct Christian assemblies, and to follow them up in the classroom. Whether your school is a Local Authority, Church Voluntary Controlled, Grant Maintained, Church Voluntary Aided, Private, or Special Agreement school this book of Christian assemblies is for you!

Christian worship in school

Christian worship in school is a requirement of the 1988 Education Reform Act, and all schools, whatever the constituent make-up of their pupils, will want to include Christian worship as part of their assemblies. *Christian Assemblies for Primary Schools* is written in the belief that worship can be stimulating, great fun and essentially thought-provoking. It offers ideas based on a wide selection of biblical material (not just those usually offered to children), and embraces different Christian viewpoints.

Many schools have a Christian foundation, and for them it must be an important concern to offer Christian (and in some cases denominational) worship to their pupils. Each school will of course wish to adapt the material offered to suit their own circumstances.

This book offers material primarily for Keystage Two pupils. While the 'school assemblies' are aimed at all the school (including teachers and/or parents), some language may need adapting to make it simpler for younger children who are present. Many of the other assemblies could also be used with Keystage One pupils providing there is some imaginative adapting of the material.

There are ten themes in the book, and each theme is explored through five different acts of collective worship, either for the whole school or for individual classes (or year groups). The themes offered are those that are to be found in the National Curriculum and will be familiar to teachers through their work in a variety of subjects.

Christian Assemblies for Primary Schools uses the term 'assembly' rather than 'collective worship' (as coined in the Education Reform Act 1988), since most teachers still use the word assembly when referring to school worship. Obviously schools 'assemble' for a number of reasons, worship being only one of these; however, in this book 'assembly' means 'worship'.

Classroom work and worship

For teachers to get the best out of this book, some thought will need to be given to worship and its relation to classroom work.

Christian worship in a school can, and should, be suitable for the age of the pupils. It should also spring from work already being carried out, or initiate new work—across the whole range of the curriculum. It cannot occur in isolation from the rest of the day, despite it being carried out in 'non-contact time'. Neither can worship take the place of Religious Education, though it can initiate Religious Education.

Each assembly, therefore, has suggestions for follow-up work in the classroom. It is certainly not envisaged that teachers will want to follow up all the suggestions, nor should they replace carefully planned schemes of work. But many teachers may find their imagination sparked so that the theme for the day moves from the assembly into the classroom; they will be able to pick up some of the ideas and weave them into work already planned.

As many teachers will know, Ofsted inspectors, as well as those conducting Section 13 Denominational Inspections, are looking for evidence that both collective worship and Religious Education nourishes the cultural, moral and spiritual development of all pupils. *Christian Assemblies for Primary Schools* will enhance such growth since the assemblies seek to foster the links between worship and the curriculum.

Worship ethos

Lastly, it must be said that no act of worship will occur if the scene is not set in an appropriate manner. Use of candles, a cross or flowers, or suitable music can offer an important focus. Considerable thought is needed as to when notices are given, since this can ruin the feel of any service, particularly if it includes some kind of complaint against pupils. A period of silence after pupils have entered the assembly area can also be very useful, to create a distinct separation between entrance or notices and worship.

With the introduction of legislation that allowed acts of worship to take place at different times of the day, in different places and in different groups, schools should make use of this opportunity to experiment with conducting worship in a number of ways. It might be worth considering, for instance, whether early morning is really the best time for classroom worship, when the teacher is engaged in doing a multiplicity of other tasks. Perhaps time at the end or middle of the day would be preferable.

The act of collective worship can, and should, be the best part of any school day. The joys and concerns of the school, and the world, should be allowed to permeate the worship, and this in its turn should infect the whole of school life. An ideal, perhaps, but one worth trying to achieve.

OURSELVES

The five assemblies offered this week seek to help pupils and staff establish a firm foundation on which to continue their spiritual growth. Before we can understand other people we have to try and understand ourselves and we must acknowledge that sometimes all is not right!

Starting again (school assembly)

We are not perfect. Very often we do and say things which make us ashamed. We might wish to go back to the beginning and start again, but how is this possible? This assembly looks at how we might start afresh.

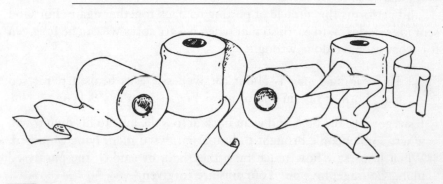

Talk about the things we do which are wrong. Encourage pupils to see that *everyone* is ashamed of what they do at some time or other. Carry out a *secret* straw-poll, by asking pupils and staff to 'close their eyes and put up their hand' if they have done any of the following recently (if they are being honest everyone will put up a hand):

- told a lie
- had nasty thoughts about someone else
- been unkind
- not helped someone.

Speak about the difficulties of trying to start again when we have just made a mess of the day, and of those times when we have felt ashamed of what we have done. Sympathize, and try to show just how difficult it is to start again.

Take a new toilet roll and undo the end. Give it to a child to hold, preferably one sitting at the end of a row. Undo the roll slowly and 'wrap up' the whole school by taking the paper around the outside rows of seated pupils until the end of the roll is reached. Be careful not to pull the paper too tightly at the corners or it will tear.

When the paper has run out, ask if anyone thinks that they can wrap the roll of paper up again, *exactly* as it was at the beginning. Allow a volunteer to try, even though it is an impossible task.

———

Remind everyone that it is very difficult to 'put yourself back' to the beginning and start again. We all do things wrong occasionally, and when we do, we are just like the toilet roll—a right mess!

However, we are luckier than the toilet roll—we *can* start again! All we have to do is say 'I'm sorry'—perhaps to the person we hurt *and* then to God, and be sure we mean it.

God performs the miracle of putting us back together again. For God sent his son, Jesus, to earth so that when we are sorry we can be forgiven for what we have done wrong.

The reading today is about forgiveness. Jesus heals a paralysed man, both of his sin and of his sickness: Matthew 9.1–8:

Jesus got into the boat and went back across the lake to his own town, where some people brought to him a paralysed man, lying on a bed. When Jesus saw how much faith they had, he said to the paralysed man, 'Courage, my son! Your sins are forgiven.'

Then some teachers of the Law said to themselves, 'This man is speaking blasphemy!'

Jesus perceived what they were thinking, so he said, 'Why are you thinking such evil things? Is it easier to say, "Your sins are forgiven," or to say, "Get up and walk"? I will prove to you, then, that the Son of Man has authority on earth to forgive sins.' So he said to the paralysed man, 'Get up, pick up your bed, and go home!'

The man got up and went home. When the people saw it, they were afraid, and praised God for giving such authority to men.

'Lead me from death to life' (*BBC Complete Come and Praise* 140)

Create a litany of confession. You might wish to prepare this in RE beforehand and use pictures or slides to accompany the confession.

Leader: Lord, we are sorry that we so often forget you. Please
   All: forgive us and help us.
Leader: Lord, we are sorry that we are unkind and thoughtless. Please
   All: forgive us and help us.
Leader: Lord, we are sorry that we _____.

RE

Continue exploring the concepts of confession and forgiveness: encourage pupils to write down some confessions, then take them outside and burn them. Read the story of the Lost Son (Luke 15.11–24 or 32), whose father not only forgave him, but came out to meet him half-way.

English

Take one sin that pupils might identify with—lying—and in groups brainstorm 'The lie!', concentrating particularly on what it feels like to tell a lie. Then follow this up by writing haikus on the subject. A haiku is a form of Japanese poetry usually based on an experience. It only has three lines, made up of 5, 7 and 5 syllables. Encourage pupils to be spontaneous and not to worry about the form. The haiku is about *feeling*. Here is an example:

> Gut-wrenching heart-beats,
> My mind numbly rejecting,
> Did I just say that?

Science

As part of work on the environment, explore the ways that humans can damage their locality. Conduct a survey of rubbish found in and around school, or take water samples from a number of different sites and sort identify indicator species to assess pollution levels.

IT

Enter the information collected on pollution into a database for retrieval at a later date.

Our Charter (class assembly)

Do we have a right to do anything we want in this world? This assembly considers what are the rights of all God's children.

Explain that the class are going to make a 'Children's Charter'. Talk about what a charter is (e.g., the Patient's Charter), and then put up a heading 'Our Charter' on the board or over-head projector. Add a selection of phrases from which the class can *choose* and take any more suggestions given. For example:

I HAVE THE RIGHT TO:

shout	be quiet
laugh	lie
scream	be listened to
steal	believe in God
say nasty things about others	pray
be silent	speak

Allow pupils to choose the phrases they desire, then point out that each of these rights will affect the rights of others. If half the class have the right to shout, this will affect the rights of the other half to be quiet! Ask whether they might wish to change any of the rights on the board.

Finally, encourage the class to see that rights also bring obligations: each right brings the obligation to respect other people's rights. If it is *their* right to live in silence, then they are obliged to be quiet for *others* for whom silence is also a right.

Note: The charter could be completed over one or two class assemblies.

 Jesus gave his disciples (and us), a charter for living. It is called the Great Commandment. Matthew 22.34–39:

When the Pharisees heard that Jesus had silenced the Sadducees, they came together, and one of them, a teacher of the Law, tried to trap him with a question.

'Teacher,' he asked, 'which is the greatest commandment in the Law?'

Jesus answered, ' "Love the Lord your God with all your heart, with all your soul, and with all your mind." This is the greatest and the most important commandment. The second most important commandment is like it: "Love your neighbour as you love yourself." The whole Law of Moses and the teachings of the prophets depend on these two commandments.'

We are very selfish people! Often we only think about ourselves. Think how often we say 'I want!', rather than 'We want!'

In one way there's nothing wrong with thinking about ourselves. After all we have to keep ourselves warm, and see that we eat and sleep enough. Other people cannot eat or sleep for us, can they? So we do have to think about ourselves.

Often it is difficult to know what is right or wrong. But Jesus had a very helpful way of reminding us. He said we should *love our neighbour* (that is, all those around us) *like ourselves*. As we have seen from the Charter, we are all different, but if we treat everyone else in the way that we would like to be treated, we won't go far wrong.

Light a candle to focus attention, and ask pupils to think back over the past 24 hours and to use their thoughts as the basis for silent, personal prayer. For example:

Lord God

I am sorry for calling my friend names, and for being rude to my Mum.

Please forgive me, and help me try to live as you would want.

Amen.

Lord God,
All too often we only think about ourselves.
Forgive us when we forget other people and trample on their feelings,
Help us to remember that you taught us to love you, ourselves, *and* other people.   Amen.

RE
Another charter for living is found in the Old Testament. Look up the Ten Commandments (Exodus 20.1–17), and discuss how helpful they are today. Look at some of the laws to help the poor and outcast (e.g., Leviticus 25). Alternatively, invite a Jewish person to speak to the class about how they observe the Law of Moses.

Art
A charter might look something like a certificate. Examine some certificates, looking at their colour, pattern, shape and printing. Make copies of the class charter experimenting with different styles. Review work, and display.

Music
As the class are thinking about one another, sing 'When I needed a neighbour, were you there?' (*BBC Complete Come and Praise* 65), or learn the Taizé song 'Mandatum Novum', which means 'I give you a new Commandment'.

Useless coins (class assembly)

Often we put on a 'nice face' and appear charming to other people, but underneath we can be very different. This assembly looks at whether we are always as nice inside as we appear.

Collect some coins no longer in circulation, e.g., 1d, ½d, 3d, 6d, 2s, or 1s. Allow pupils to examine the coins. Talk about their face value, and what items could be purchased with them in the past? Look at coins in current use. Discuss what they might purchase now.

Every country replaces its currency from time to time. The coins eventually become old and dirty and the edges get rubbed smooth. Sometimes countries decide to change all their money and bring in another system. This happened in 1971 in Great Britain when decimal currency was introduced. When this happens:

- old coins are no longer useful;
- machines taking money must be changed to accept new coins;
- old money can only be changed at banks;
- old coins still look OK, but they cannot be used.

Jesus knew a lot about people who seemed to look all right on the outside. He taught that it is not good enough to look good. It is important to *think* and *act* in the same way.

In other words, it is no good saying one thing but doing another. If we do that, we are like a disused coin; it looks acceptable, but it cannot be used and therefore it is not much good.

In this story Jesus speaks of a Pharisee and a tax collector. Luke 18.10–14:

'Once there were two men who went up to the Temple to pray: one was a Pharisee, the other a tax collector.

'The Pharisee stood apart by himself and prayed, "I thank you, God, that I am not greedy, dishonest, or an adulterer, like that tax collector over there. I fast two days a week, and I give you a tenth of all my income."

'But the tax collector stood at a distance and would not even raise his face to heaven, but beat on his breast and said, "God, have pity on me, a sinner!" I tell you,' said Jesus, 'the tax collector, and not the Pharisee, was in the right with God when he went home.'

Give each pupil a flower (either wild or cultivated) and ask them to spend a moment in silence examining their particular flower. Ask them to notice all they can about their flower. Notice, for instance, that in this case it is as beautiful inside as outside.

Finally, pupils might like to ask God to make them as 'attractive inside as they are outside'.

Lord God,
Help us to see that the way we think
   is just as important as the way we act.
Help us to have lovely, beautiful thoughts
   so that what we think and what we say may be the same.   Amen.

Art

Continue looking at the idea of outsides and insides being different by cutting open some apples (horizontally). Make sure windfalls are included; draw the 'hidden' insides. Alternatively, use the inside of the apples for print-making.

RE

Follow up the assembly and the artwork by discussing 'insides and outsides'. What is important is not how we (or others) *look* but what sort of persons we *are*. How can we know this? Organize an 'unwanted coins' collection for charity. (Notice even unwanted coins have a use!)

History

If suitable, make a study of coins as part of work on your core unit of History.

Maths
Collect coins from different monetary systems. Sort and classify according to different criteria (e.g., size, colour, number). Record the data on charts.

Firm foundations (school assembly)

The Bible teaches us that it is important to build our lives on firm foundations, so that at the first difficulty things do not fall apart.

Before the assembly draw some pictures on large sheets of sugar paper. Hang a washing line across the room and peg these onto it as you tell the story of the 'Two house builders'. Pictures needed:

- Two workmen in modern clothes.
- A house built on rock, well above the stream.
- A house built on sand, right near the river.
- The two houses with rain falling, and lightning in the sky.
- River overflowing and entering the second house, still raining.
- House built on sand collapsing, and other house safe.

9

Jesus tells his disciples the story of the two house builders. Matthew 7.24–27:

'Anyone who hears these words of mine and obeys them is like a wise man who built his house on rock. The rain poured down, the rivers overflowed, and the wind blew hard against that house. But it did not fall, because it was built on rock.

'But anyone who hears these words of mine and does not obey them is like a foolish man who built his house on sand. The rain poured down, the rivers overflowed, the wind blew hard against that house, and it fell. And what a terrible fall that was!'

Jesus said that we are like the house built on rock if we listen to his words and obey them. But if we do not obey his words, then we are like the house built on sand. When troubles came, the house collapsed.

When we listen to his words and obey them—for example, to love and help one another—then we are like the house built on safe ground. No matter how bad things became, it stood safe; and when things get difficult in our lives, God will look after us.

Lord God,
Help us to listen to Jesus' command to love you
    and to follow your teaching.
So that, like the house built on rock,
    we are kept safe from harm
    and protected from all evil.   Amen.

'The wise man built his house upon the rock' (*Junior Praise* 252)

Art
Using the story of the two houses as a basis, create 'stained glass' pictures out of coloured tissue paper and black sugar paper. Hang at a window.

Music
Explore sounds with a variety of tuned and untuned instruments to reflect the story of the two houses. Select and organize these into a whole composition, and record as appropriate. Tell the story again, this time accompanied by music.

RE
Look at the foundations of the Jewish faith: God's Covenant with Abraham (Genesis 17.1–8); the Shema prayer (Deuteronomy 6.1–9). Find out about the tephilin worn by Orthodox Jews.

Geography
Look at rivers: e.g., size, sources, tributaries, river flooding, and erosion.

Science
Alternatively, explore the force and motion associated with water, and water as a source of energy. Visit a water-mill; or find out about the moon and its effect on tides.

Design and technology
Design a water-wheel out of suitable material. In groups, plan and make simple water-wheels. Evaluate the end product.

I agree! (school assembly)

This assembly looks at the fact that we are all responsible for making our own decisions, and for standing by them.

Invite a few pupils to play a game. Inform them that one wall in the room is the 'Yes!' wall and one wall is the 'No!' wall.

Then ask a series of questions and invite the volunteers to stand near whichever wall suits their answer. The space between the two walls is anything from 'Yes' to 'No'. For instance, if you ask 'Do you like ice-cream?', those who like it only a little should stand just over half way between the two walls. Encourage the pupils to be very honest.

Questions might include:

Do you like sweets?	Do you like pear drops?
Do you like rain?	Do you like going to the dentist?
Do you like coming to school?	Do you like Games/PE?

At the end, ask the pupils to sit down, and thank them for their help.

Point out that each child had to make their own decisions. They could not just follow their friend. Each one was responsible for their own answer, and for exactly where they stood.

All too often we try to follow other people and do what they do, whether or not we want to. But God doesn't want us to follow each other like sheep. He wants us to decide things for ourselves, and if we make mistakes to be big enough and brave enough not to say 'Someone else made me!'

Each one of us is so different that we must decide what *we* want to do and how *we* want to live. At the end of the day, we are responsible to God for everything we decide and for everything we do.

In this story Jesus says we are like trees. Good trees (or good people) have good fruit and bad trees have bad fruit. Matthew 12.33–36:

'To have good fruit you must have a healthy tree; if you have a poor tree, you will have bad fruit. A tree is known by the kind of fruit it bears. You snakes—how can you say good things when you are evil? For the mouth speaks what the heart is full of. A good person brings good things out of his treasure of good things; a bad person brings bad things out of his treasure of bad things.

'You can be sure that on Judgement Day everyone will have to give account of every useless word he has ever spoken.'

'The journey of life' (*BBC Complete Come and Praise* 45)

Lord God,
Help us to remember that we must stand alone before you,
    and that we are responsible for ourselves.
We cannot blame others when we do things wrong.
We must stand on our feet and take the blame ourselves.
Help us to know what is right and what is wrong,
    and to make the right decisions.   Amen.

RE
After the assembly, look at the idea of confession—of being responsible for our mistakes. What do different Christian denominations say about this (e.g., the 'mercy seat', the sacrament of confession)?

Art
Look at a copy of Rembrandt's picture of the cavalier boy before the Roundheads, titled 'And when did you last see your father?'. (This boy had to make his own decision!)

English
Talk about owning up, then read *Bully for you*, illustrated by Toni Goffe, which encourages children to own up to bullying.

Week 2

OTHERS

This week's assembly theme considers other people. Pupils and staff are encouraged to put themselves in other people's shoes and to examine questions like 'How can I help?' and 'What do they really need from me?'

Other people's shoes (school assembly)

If we put ourselves in someone else's shoes we have to think about other people, and not just about ourselves. God says when we do this it is as though we are doing it for him.

Collect a variety of different shoes that might conceivably belong to *two* people who are connected with the school. Be as inventive as possible, and do not inform the pupils that the shoes belong only to two people.

Woman	Man
ballet shoes	football boots
wellington boots	walking boots
slippers	city shoes
town shoes	flippers

dancing shoes	waders
Doc Martins	plimsolls
beach shoes	flip-flops

Ask pupils to describe people who might own such shoes. Come to some conclusions about the owners, and put these up on a board or over-head projector.

The pupils might decide that the shoes are worn by a variety of people of different ages and occupations. Finally, own up—they belong to only two people. You could produce the two people concerned if you have used real people.

There is a famous phrase which says 'I wouldn't want to be in your shoes.' It means I wouldn't want to be you at the moment! This week we *are* going to be in each other's shoes, however. We are going to look at other people and find out what they do, how they feel, and what they want.

Much of the day however we walk around thinking only of ourselves— we don't really examine other people in great detail. For example, can you remember what your mother or your sister or brother wore yesterday? Did they look tired, or happy, or what?

We need to learn to look at other people (those in our class, our family, our neighbours) in this careful way, so that we can really help them. This is the way that God cares for us. He knows exactly how we feel and what we need, and he gives us just what is right for us.

Jesus taught that we must help as many people as we can. He also said that when we care for others it is just as though we were caring for him. Matthew 25.34b–40:

'"Come, you that are blessed by my Father! Come and possess the kingdom which has been prepared for you ever since the creation of the world. I was hungry and you fed me, thirsty and you gave me a drink; I was a stranger and you received me in your homes, naked and you clothed me; I was sick and you took care of me, in prison and you visited me."

'The righteous will then answer him, "When, Lord, did we ever see you hungry and feed you, or thirsty and give you a drink? When did we ever see you a stranger and welcome you in our homes, or naked and clothe you? When did we ever see you sick or in prison, and visit you?"

15

The King will reply, "I tell you, whenever you did this for one of the least important of these brothers of mine, you did it for me."'

 Lord God,
Help us to see people as they really are,
    to observe those who are tired or ill
    and to see the sad and the lonely.
Teach us how to care for other people as you care for us,
    and help us learn to walk in other people's shoes.   Amen.

 'When I needed a neighbour, were you there?' (*BBC Complete Come and Praise* 65)

→ *Maths*
Continue thinking about shoes and feet by exploring pupils' different foot sizes. Or take 'foot-measurements' of the playground or classroom.

RE
Look at the work of someone who could be said to fulfil Jesus' commands to look after those who need help (e.g., a hospital chaplain, a hospice nurse, a prison chaplain). What ways might pupils help other people?

English
As a way of observing other people, try 'walking in each other's shoes', that is, copying each other's walks. What does it teach you about others? Write some creative work entitled 'Your shoes'.

PE
Alternatively, in pairs, copy each other's dance movements.

The wish list (class assembly)

We usually know exactly what *we* want if someone wishes to give us a present, but do we always know what other people want?

As a class, or alone, create a 'wish list' of about five items. Pupils may be as selfish as they desire. A list might look like this:

When this is done, ask pupils to make a similar list but for a friend (which could be shorter). At this stage, they should not confer with each other, but must guess what the other person would prefer. Do not allow too much time for the task.

Lastly, as a class, create a 'wish list' for a child living in a country where there is famine or war. Are there any differences between the lists?

 Jesus taught people to love other people as they 'love themselves'. Part of loving one another is trying to put ourselves in their place and to imagine what their life might be like, and what they might need. It is no good wishing to give a child in a very poor country a pair of skates when they really want clean water. Neither is it any good giving someone else what *we* would like for ourselves; we must give them what *they* want. That is how we would like others to treat us.

 In this reading St Paul speaks of the way we should love other people. 1 Corinthians 13.4–7:

Love is patient and kind; it is not jealous or conceited or proud; love is not ill-mannered or selfish or irritable; love does not keep a record of wrongs; love is not happy with evil, but is happy with the truth. Love never gives up; and its faith, hope, and patience never fail.

 Lord God,
Help us to love other people as we love ourselves,
    so that we find out what they really need and want.
We pray for children who have no food or water,
    for those who have no parents and who are afraid,
    and for those for whom the future is bleak.
Let us never forget all those who need our help
    and our prayers.   Amen.

➡ *RE*
Follow up the 'wish list' for a child from a country suffering from famine or war. Find out about projects that endeavour to improve their living conditions. Look at material produced by

Christian Aid, Tear Fund or the Leprosy Mission for primary schools (see Useful Addresses). Organize an event to raise money, or awareness, for one of these causes.

Geography
As part of the Geography syllabus continue to learn more about the contrasting locality looked at in the assembly.

English
Read *Giving* by Shirley Hughes, which continues to explore the idea of giving to other people.

Art
Thinking about others, paint a picture for someone else—a scene or style that they would really enjoy.

Listening to others (class assembly)

Continuing the idea of putting ourselves in others' shoes, this assembly thinks about how we listen to other people.

 Divide the class into groups of about eight pupils, and give each group a ball of wool. Inform them there are very few rules to this game other than the following:

- Whoever holds the ball should talk (e.g., about going on holiday, playing with the dog, watching television).
- If you do not have the ball you *must not* talk.
- When the time is up, throw the ball to another person, but keep hold of the end of wool. The group will gradually become criss-crossed in wool.
- You will call 'time' (allow a minute or so for each speaker).

Talk about the game. Did pupils find it difficult? Did they want to talk when they no longer had the ball? Did they want to join in and say 'I like that too!'? Did they spend all the time thinking about what they were going to say, instead of listening to the other person? Did they find they were looking at the person holding the ball, or not?

Comment that the theme this week is 'Others', and one of the nicest things we can do for other people is to listen to them really carefully. When we listen to people we need to concentrate with *all* of our mind, instead of pretending to listen and actually thinking about something else. Also, we need to look at them. There is always time to have our say later. The important thing is to give all our attention to the other person who is speaking.

After all, if we never practise listening to each other, we shall never be able to hear God when he speaks to us!

The writer of this psalm speaks about God, who listens to his people. Psalm 116.1–7:

I love the Lord, because he hears me;
   he listens to my prayers.
He listens to me
   every time I call to him.

The danger of death was all around me;
   the horrors of the grave closed in on me;
   I was filled with fear and anxiety.
Then I called to the Lord,
   'I beg you, Lord, save me!'

The Lord is merciful and good;
   our God is compassionate.
The Lord protects the helpless;
   when I was in danger, he saved me.
Be confident, my heart,
   because the Lord has been good to me.

Encourage 'active prayer' by getting pupils into pairs to talk about things they may wish to pray for—one to speak and one to listen. Then reverse the roles. Finally, close the prayer time with a few simple words, e.g., 'Lord God, we offer you our prayers and ask you to hear them. Amen.'
Alternatively, use this prayer:

Lord God,
Help us to learn to listen carefully to one another,
   so that we forget ourselves
   and only remember other people.
Help us also to learn to listen to you
   so that we can hear you when you call us.   Amen.

English
Continue to develop pupils' listening skills, by trying another listening exercise. For example, divide the class into threes. One person is to speak, one to listen and one to observe. Ask the *speaker* to talk on any simple subject (e.g., my dog/Mum etc.). After a moment or two, the *listener* should report back to the *speaker* exactly what they have said. At the end, the *observer* reports back on anything they have noticed (e.g., X leaned forward to listen better, or looked away, or appeared to day-dream). Their job is to report what they notice. Debrief the class afterwards on what it felt like to talk, to listen, and to observe.

Music
Still concentrating on listening skills, play a cd or tape of a well-known piece of music, for example, *The Planets* by Holst (Mars or Venus Suite). Afterwards get the pupils to write down their feelings about the music.

RE
Now listen using the 'mind's eye'. Tell a story from the Bible in the form of a guided meditation. Encourage pupils to close their eyes and to sit comfortably. Carry out a relaxation exercise if desired, then tell the story *in your own words*, so that the pupils can picture the scene and imagine they are actually present. The following stories would be suitable:

- The lost sheep: Luke 15:1–7
- The lost coin: Luke 15:8–10
- Jesus calms a storm: Luke 8:22–25.

Allow the pupils to come gently back to the present.

Sharing with others (school or class assembly)

Sometimes we have to share things with other people, and we may find this very hard. This assembly looks at sharing not just ordinary things, but also those things that are very precious to us.

Using an over-head projector or board, talk about things that are important or precious to us. You may like to explain the word 'precious' as 'something that is very, very special to us'.

Ask what things are precious to pupils and make a list of their suggestions. These might include:

my teddy bear	my bicycle
a box of special belongings	money in my piggy bank
a picture of my Nan	my skates

Write up all suggestions.

This is the story of a boy who lived many years ago, and who had something very special to share with Jesus. John 6.1–13:

Jesus went across Lake Galilee (or, Lake Tiberias, as it is also called). A large crowd followed him, because they had seen his miracles of healing those who were ill. Jesus went up a hill and sat down with his disciples. The time for the Passover Festival was near. Jesus looked round and saw that a large crowd was coming to him, so he asked Philip, 'Where can we buy enough food to feed all these people?' (He said this to test Philip; actually he already knew what he would do.)

Philip answered, 'For everyone to have even a little, it would take more than two hundred silver coins to buy enough bread.'

Another of his disciples, Andrew, who was Simon Peter's brother said, 'There is a boy here who has five loaves of barley bread and two fish. But they will certainly not be enough for all these people.'

'Make the people sit down,' Jesus told them. (There was a lot of grass there.) So all the people sat down; there were about five thousand of them. Jesus took the bread, gave thanks to God, and distributed it to the people who were sitting there. He did the same with the fish, and they all had as much as they wanted. When they were all full, he said to his disciples, 'Gather the pieces left over; let us not waste any.' So they gathered them all up and filled twelve baskets with the pieces left over from the five barley loaves which the people had eaten.

(For school assembly.)
'I will bring to you' (*BBC Complete Come and Praise* 59)

23

We might not think that the boy's gift was very important. But the five tiny loaves (more like rolls really), and two small fish were probably very important to him. His mother would have got up really early in the morning to bake the rolls, and his father would have gone out to catch the fish on the Sea of Galilee. There was no deep-freeze to keep the food fresh, so it had to be baked or caught each day. The boy gave Jesus all that he had.

We have just been talking about things that are special to us. 'Suppose I asked you to give them away, to help someone else—I wonder if you could do it? Now, I do not want you to give away all your precious things, certainly not without your parents' permission, but I do want you to think about how hard it might be to give things away that are very precious to you.'

However, sometimes we have to give away some of what we have to other people. For instance, as a country we have to share our food with people in developing countries like Africa, where many adults and children have little food. We also have to share our education and our skills—how to drill for clean water, how to stop children from getting illnesses caused by dirt, and how to read and write. Often we have to share our money with others, too, or, as with the boy in the story, we share whatever we have, no matter how precious it is.

Lord God,
We thank you for all the things that are precious to us.
Help us to know when we must share with others,
    and to offer our gifts gladly and willingly
    knowing that this is work you call us to do.   Amen.

RE
Continuing the idea of sharing with others, look at the work of Tear Fund, UNICEF, Christian Aid, Oxfam or CAFOD (see Useful Addresses at the end of the book). All of these aid agencies produce material suitable for use in primary schools.

History
During the nineteenth century there were many people who gave money and time to help the poor. If the class is studying Victorian

Britain find out about any nineteenth-century reformer (e.g., Shaftesbury and the climbing boys).

Geography
Compare the economy of the area in which your school is situated to that of a similar area in a developing country. How does this affect daily life? For example, what goods and services are provided? What is the land used for?

Trusting others (school or class assembly)

Much of our life is lived with other people in community, and we have to learn to trust one another. This assembly reminds us that we also have to learn to trust in God.

With the help of at least ten pupils (or as many as space permits) conduct a 'lap sit'. Ensure that the pupils stand one in front of the other (not sideways) in a very tight circle. Each child should be virtually touching the other, with no space between them.

At a given signal ask all the children to bend their knees and sit on each other's laps—in other words, to trust each other that there is a 'seat'. If all sit at the same time they will sit on each other's laps.

When they have achieved this, remind them that there is nothing holding them up except each other.

When those conducting the lap-sit have returned to their places pick up the idea of trust. The people doing the lap-sit had to trust each other. If one of them had made a mistake the whole circle would have come crashing down.

Trust is one of the earliest things that we learn. A baby learns to trust that its mother will feed her and keep her warm, and in the first few years of her life, that daylight will return each morning and the sun will shine. Trust is something we all learn about very quickly.

From our first days, then, we have to trust other people. Sometimes our trust is misplaced, people let us down, and we have to learn to trust again. As with the lap-sit, we have to keep on putting our trust in other people, and not worry that they might let us down.

The Bible teaches us that there is only one person who will never let us down. There is only one person in whom we can put all our trust, and that is God. God always looks after us and cares for us, God will not let us down.

 In our reading today Jesus speaks about trusting in God. God will give us all that we need in this life. Luke 12.22–31:

Then Jesus said to the disciples, 'And so I tell you not to worry about the food you need to stay alive or about the clothes you need for your body. Life is much more important than food, and the body much more important than clothes. Look at the crows: they don't sow seeds or gather a harvest; they don't have store-rooms or barns; God feeds them! You are worth so much more than birds! Can any of you live a bit longer by worrying about it? If you can't manage even such a small thing, why worry about the other things? Look how the wild flowers grow: they don't work or make clothes for themselves. But I tell you that not even King Solomon with all his wealth had clothes as beautiful as one of these flowers. It is God who clothes the wild grass—grass that is here today and gone tomorrow, burnt up in the oven. Won't he be all the more sure to clothe you? How little faith you have!

'So don't be all upset, always concerned about what you will eat and drink. (For the pagans of this world are always concerned about all these things.) Your Father knows that you need these things. Instead, be concerned with his Kingdom, and he will provide you with these things.'

(For school assembly.)
'There are hundreds of sparrows' (BBC Complete Come and Praise 15)

Hand out small circles of paper and ask pupils to write the words 'I trust you' and to draw a smiling 'friendship' face on one side. The teacher should do the same.

When these have been completed, gather them up and place in a bowl. Then give them out again so that each person has another face. Spend the last moment in silence looking at the friendship circle. Encourage everyone to ask God, in the silence of their heart, to help them to trust others *and* to trust God.

➡ RE
Conduct a lap-sit with the whole class of pupils, perhaps in the playground. Alternatively try other 'trust games' (e.g., blindfold someone and lead them through an obstacle course). Talk about trust and how we feel when we are let down.

English
Continuing the theme of trust, create some role-play about a child let down by a friend.

History
If the class are working on the study unit Britain since 1930, interview members of the community about those they had to trust during the Second World War.

PE
Play a team game that requires trust, or hold a relay race and emphasize the need to trust members of the team to do their best.

Week 3

COMMUNITY

This week's theme explores the notion of community: the different community groups that pupils will belong to, as well as some of the tensions that cause difficulties for communities. These assemblies explore the Christian idea of community, and its new dimension.

Mapping our communities (school assembly)

The theme this week is community. An easy way of describing a community is to say that it is a group of people who have something in common with each other. We all belong to many such groups.

From information given to you by pupils and staff create a 'web' on an over-head projector or board to show how many different groups they belong to.

As you will see, we all belong to many communities, and we know very many people. All of these groups are very different from one another.

However, these groups do have one thing in common: all the people that belong to them have the same interest. In a stamp club everyone enjoys collecting stamps, and in a drama club all the members enjoy putting on plays.

It is the same with another community that we all belong to—our family. We usually have the same surname and live in the same house. We go on holiday together, we eat together, and we spend Christmas with each other. However, we do not always have to be together or like the same things to be a family. We are still a family even when we may be apart or when we prefer doing different things.

Another community to which we all belong is this school. We may be different ages, and in different classes, but we are all members of this community.

 Our reading today is about the beginning of a new community. God calls Abram and his family to be his people, and in doing so he changes his name from Abram to Abraham. Genesis 12.1–3:

The Lord said to Abram, 'Leave your country, your relatives, and your father's home, and go to a land that I am going to show you. I will give you many descendants, and they will become a great nation. I will bless you and make your name famous, so that you will be a blessing.

'I will bless those who bless you, but I will curse those who curse you. And through you I will bless all the nations.'

 Lord God,
We pray for all the communities to which we belong.
We remember their leaders and members,
   and especially we pray for our local church(es).
We thank you for our families, and for our school.
We pray especially for those who are ill
   and who cannot be with us today in this community.   Amen.

'You can build a wall around you' (*BBC Complete Come and Praise* 91)

➡️ *RE*
Follow up the assembly by making a list of all the people who 'belong' to the school (e.g., cleaners, pupils, governors, lollipop person, teachers, secretary). Then create a wall display, preferably with photographs, for the school entrance hall, with a large title: 'Members of our school community'. Make a school intercession list from this information and use at appropriate assemblies.

History
Continue looking at the school community by researching into the history of the school. Create a time-line of the school showing the changes that have occurred over the years.

English
Members of many communities wear a uniform. In small groups, discuss the wearing of a school uniform. Is it necessary? Does it help a sense of belonging? Marshal the arguments for and against the wearing of a school uniform.

Art
In pairs, observe each other and make likenesses of each other using a variety of media. Display under the title 'We belong to Class ____'.

Design and technology
In small groups examine the present school uniform and design a new school uniform for the twenty-first century.

IT
Store and update information on the school intercessions list made in RE.

Community conflict (class assembly)

This assembly looks at the way we live in community and at the rules we need to live in harmony with each other.

Communities—like schools, families and churches—are made up of many people, and because of this there are times when there are struggles in the group. We might have many things in common, for instance we might all like football or swimming and want our club to win the trophy for the year, but we might have different ideas as to how we should do that.

This is all quite normal, though often we have to sit down and talk about what the whole group wants, and decide on some rules. But it is not normal when communities fight one another, or when there is no peace in a family or community group.

Jesus reminded us what will happen if a community is divided. Luke 11.14–17:

Jesus was driving out a demon that could not talk; and when the demon went out, the man began to talk. The crowds were amazed, but some of the people said, 'It is Beelzebul, the chief of the demons, who gives him the power to drive them out.'

Others wanted to trap Jesus, so they asked him to perform a miracle to show that God approved of him. But Jesus knew what they were thinking, so he said to them, 'Any country that divides itself into groups which fight each other will not last very long; a family divided against itself falls apart.'

Talk about why rules are needed. What might happen if there were no rules in school, or in society?

Then make a list of written and unwritten rules that apply to school.

Close the assembly by reminding the pupils that their class is a community. One way of making sure that any community is happy is to ask for God's peace to be on everyone in the community. The Peace is one of the oldest parts of worship in many Christian services.

Either say the words of the Peace to the whole class, or encourage them to say it to one another:

First person: The peace of the Lord be always with you.
Second person: And also with you.

RE
Follow up the work on rules in assembly by looking at the Ten Commandments (Exodus 20.1–17). Then look at Jesus' commandment (Matthew 22.34–40). Apply Jesus' words to some situations in the news, or within school.

Music
Think about harmony and rules, and apply to music. For example, create a simple musical rhythm then gradually introduce a new theme.

Geography
What rules apply to space within the school? Carry out a physical survey of the school, observing and recording information. Identify areas used by different groups.

English
Create some role-play about rules, or the lack of them, in the playground. Or explore conflict within the family and make up some role-play about choosing a TV programme.

God's family (school assembly)

This assembly continues the theme of community by looking at the Church, that is, God's family.

As we have seen, we belong to many different communities and groups: our family, different clubs, this school. And if we have been baptized, we also belong to another community, to God's family, the Church.

If we were baptized as a baby then our parents 'gave us to God' and we became members of the Christian family. We were even given a 'Christian' name. In some countries children who are baptized are given a saint's name, and have an extra birthday or 'name' day on their special saint's day.

But God's family doesn't just include all those children and adults who have been baptized and who are alive now; it also includes all those Christians who have died in the past. The Christian family is a very big family! Here are just some of the people who belong to God's family.

Prepare a short presentation about some saints or special Christians. (If possible, avoid those saints who might be said to have a doubtful history.) You might wish to dress pupils in appropriate costume. By changing the words you could have the saint accompanied by a person to speak on their behalf. The following are some suggestions, but others would be as appropriate.

ST EDMUND
'I was King of the East Angles. The Danes invaded my country in 865

AD and tried to make me a 'puppet King'. But I would have nothing to do with it, so they killed me by using me for target practice. My body was eventually moved to Bury St Edmunds.'

ELIZABETH FRY

'My family were Quakers and my father was a banker. I worked for the Quakers in the nineteenth century, and in particular with female prisoners in Newgate Prison. I founded a group that helped many women prisoners throughout Europe.'

ROBERT RAIKES

'I was a journalist working for the *Gloucester Journal*. At first I worked in prisons helping to improve the conditions there, but seeing the numbers of children left alone on a Sunday, I began to work with them. In 1780 I started a Sunday school for these children. There was a great deal of opposition, but I kept going, and soon there were Sunday schools everywhere.'

ST WENCESLAS

'I was a Prince of Bohemia, and was brought up as a Christian by my grandmother Ludmilla. However, my mother hated Christianity and when my father died she did all she could to stamp out Christianity in the country. When I became king I did all I could to promote Christianity, but I had many enemies and I was murdered on my way to mass. You may know the song about me that is still sung at Christmas.'

Many years before Jesus was born, the writer of this psalm knew all about being a member of God's family. He knew what God had done for him and was grateful. Psalm 100:

> Sing to the Lord, all the world!
>> Worship the Lord with joy;
>> come before him with happy songs!
>
> Acknowledge that the Lord is God.
>> He made us, and we belong to him;
>> we are his people, we are his flock.
>
> Enter the temple gates with thanksgiving,
>> go into its courts with praise.
>> Give thanks to him and praise him.

The Lord is good;
   his love is eternal
   and his faithfulness lasts for ever.

 Light candles in memory of the saints and other special Christians, mentioning their names as you light each candle. Alternatively, light candles for anyone you know who has died in the last year, or for a national figure, or for 'all children who have died recently'.

Lord God,
We give thanks for your family the Church,
   and for all who work for it today.
We pray for our local churches and for ——— (clergy).
We give thanks for all those who have worked for the Church
   over the centuries.
Help us never to forget their example,
   but to learn from them continually.   Amen.

'Bind us, together, Lord' (*Junior Praise* 17)

Science
Continuing the idea of families (or groups), place objects together according to recognizable features. Ask 'What makes them belong to this group?'

RE
Pick up the idea of becoming a member of God's family and look at initiation ceremonies (infant baptism, dedication and believer's baptism), and especially at the promises taken. Hold a mock baptism, or attend a baptism at your local church.

History
Visit your local cathedral (or suitable church) and find out about local saints or famous Christians associated with the area. Contact the cathedral education officer for further information.

35

Community people (school assembly)

As people living in community we have to learn to live together. This assembly reminds us that in order to make a community work we have truly to care about other people.

One of the signs that a community of people care for each other is if they notice things about each other. Often people do not have to speak to tell us something. Our eyes can tell us what they are trying to say. We are going to see how good you are at detecting messages.

Use a number of people to mime some silent actions. The volunteer (a pupil or member of staff) will need to have been forewarned. The following are only a few suggestions, and you may think of more suitable ones:

head bent, rubbing both eyes with the knuckles: *crying*
head down, shoulders and arms hanging: *miserable*

big grin:	*happy*
fists clenched, arms up above head:	*the winner*

Today's story is about a woman who did not say anything either, yet Jesus knew what she was trying to tell him. It is also about someone who seemed to welcome Jesus, but by his manner Jesus knew otherwise. Luke 7.36 39, and 44 48:

A Pharisee invited Jesus to have dinner with him, and Jesus went to his house and sat down to eat. In that town was a woman who lived a sinful life. She heard that Jesus was eating in the Pharisee's house, so she brought an alabaster jar full of perfume and stood behind Jesus, by his feet, crying and wetting his feet with her tears. Then she dried his feet with her hair, kissed them, and poured the perfume on them. When the Pharisee saw this, he said to himself, 'If this man really were a prophet, he would know who this woman is who is touching him; he would know what kind of sinful life she lives!' . . .

Then Jesus turned to the woman and said to Simon, 'Do you see this woman? I came into your home, and you gave me no water for my feet, but she has washed my feet with her tears and dried them with her hair. You did not welcome me with a kiss, but she has not stopped kissing my feet since I came. You provided no olive-oil for my head, but she has covered my feet with perfume. I tell you, then, the great love she has shown proves that her many sins have been forgiven. But whoever has been forgiven little shows only a little love.'

Then Jesus said to the woman, 'Your sins are forgiven.'

By her actions, Jesus knew what the woman was trying to say. He cared about her enough to notice all her actions. Like him, we must get good at noticing other people at home and in school. Are they happy? Are they sad? What does their face and body tell us?

Then there was Simon. We are told the Pharisee appeared to welcome Jesus into his house, but in fact he had given him a very poor welcome, not the kind of welcome given to a special guest.

Sometimes we are like Simon: our words do not match our actions. We sound friendly, but our actions are unloving. A school or a family that is a united community will want to show that it cares about everyone, not just in words, but in its actions.

'Would you walk by on the other side?' (*BBC Complete Come and Praise* 70)

 Lord God,
Please forgive the things we have done that are wrong,
 the times we have hurt others:
 pulled faces at those we know,
 turned away or frowned at friends.
Help us to match up the things we do with the things we say,
 so that our actions speak louder than our words. Amen.

RE
Follow up the assembly by making a study of *actions* in Christian worship, looking at more than one denomination (e.g., bowing the head, genuflecting, hands together and eyes closed, crossing oneself, arms raised). What do they convey? Alternatively, look at another story showing a difference between words and actions: e.g., the Pharisee and the judge (Luke 18.9–14), or the rich young man (Luke 18.18–27).

English
Read *Miles and the Computer* by Taffy Davis—a funny story about forgiveness.

Doing things together (class assembly)

This assembly explores the way that a community must work together to produce something worthwhile.

A community works or plays, together. It simply cannot be a community if it *never* meets together. It is also important that everyone is involved, because each person can do different things to help the community: for example, one person can keep the peace, another knows how to get things done.

Working together can be great fun, but it can also be very hard, especially if everyone has to agree to the decisions.

In this assembly we are going to work together to make something, and when we have finished, what we have made will not belong to just one person but will belong to everyone who helped to make it.

Create and draw 'badges' (in groups of four), to say something about the school. Decide what pictures would be suitable: for example, is the school on a hill or near a river? Is the school good at one kind of sport? Or is someone famous linked to the school?

Give each group a sheet of paper, and inform them that they must work together, making joint decisions. Each segment of the badge can be drawn by one member of the group providing the whole group have agreed on its contents. Afterwards, talk for a few minutes as a class about working together as a community or group.

The reading shows what it was like for the new Christian Church to work together. However, even they had their problems at times. Acts 2.43–47:

Many miracles and wonders were being done through the apostles, and everyone was filled with awe. All the believers continued together in close fellowship and shared their belongings with one another. They would sell their property and possessions, and distribute the money among all, according to what each one needed. Day after day they met as a group in the Temple, and they had their meals together in their homes, eating with glad and humble hearts, praising God and enjoying the good will of all the people. And every day the Lord added to their group those who were being saved.

If appropriate, link hands together to make a circle while this prayer is said. The pupils will only need to know the words 'Lord, hear us'.

Leader: Lord God,
　　　　 Help us to work together in peace.
　 All: Lord, hear us.
Leader: Help us to listen to each other in silence.
　 All: Lord, hear us.
Leader: Help us to care for each other in love.
　 All: Lord, hear us.

PE
Continue with the idea of working together and play a competitive team game that requires the support and participation of all the members of the class.

RE
Discuss how the groups managed to work together during the assembly (if this has not been done already). Did they find it difficult? Who decided what pictures to draw? Were they jointly decided by the group? Now look at instances in the Bible when people found it difficult to work together: for example, Joseph and his brothers (Genesis 37.1–8).

English
Continue looking at group conflict and harmony by role-playing

some situations: for example, deciding what to watch on television, where to go on holiday, or buying a present for Granny. Allow time for reflection and response to the improvisations.

Music
Working in small groups, write music for 'The creation of the world'. Allocate different verses from Genesis 1.1—2.3, and start with chaos, before creation and orderliness have begun. Accompany the music with a reading of the words. Analyse the results and make recommendations for improvement.

Week 4

DIVERSITY

Pupils learn about the diversity of human life and living processes in Science and in Geography. Through an exploration of what it means to be human, pupils are encouraged to learn more about their own physical and spiritual lives, and of those around them, and to use the natural diversity of creation as a basis for worship.

Our differences (school assembly)

Our theme for this week's assemblies is diversity, or differences. As we shall see, people, animals, and even countries, are all totally different from one another. It is these differences that make our world such a wonderful place!

 Conduct an investigation of different sizes among the staff and pupils. Use any means of measurement desired—a template of a foot or hand, a ruler or tape measure, a wall chart, or other non-standard measurement.

Decide the following:

- Who has the largest hands in the school?
- Who has the smallest hands?
- Who is the tallest?
- Who is the shortest?
- Who has the longest hair?

Notice how very different we are from one another. Some people have brown hair, some blond; some have blue eyes and some black. We are different heights and different sizes; we talk and act differently from one another! However, we do not just look and sound different, we are different in many other ways: in our experiences, in our feelings, in the things we are good at.

Optional:
Explore further by asking general questions of volunteers, or the whole school (and include any adults present):

- Who likes rain?
- Who has a sister?
- Who went on holiday to France/Scotland?
- Who is a noisy/quiet person?
- Who can drive a car?

Why are we all so different? Why are some of us healthy and strong, and others born with disabilities? We do not know all the answers, but one reason could be that God has different jobs for us to do. If we were all the same, we would not be able to do them, and our world would be a much poorer place.

Today's reading is a story told by Jesus. Jesus says our different gifts are like money to be used. God expects us to use everything that we have. If we are good at running, or listening to people, or singing, or simply good at being happy, then we should use these gifts. Matthew 25.14–28:

'Once there was a man who was about to go on a journey; he called his servants and put them in charge of his property. He gave to each one according to his ability: to one he gave five thousand gold coins, to another he gave two thousand, and to another he gave one thousand. Then he left on his journey. The servant who had received five thousand coins went at once and invested his money and earned another five thousand. In the same way the servant who had received two thousand coins earned another two thousand. But the servant who had received one thousand coins went off, dug a hole in the ground, and hid his master's money.

'After a long time the master of those servants came back and settled accounts with them. The servant who had received five thousand coins came in and handed over the other five thousand. "You gave me five thousand coins, sir," he said. "Look! Here are another five thousand that I have earned." "Well done, you good and faithful servant!" said his master. "You have been faithful in managing small amounts, so I will put you in charge of large amounts. Come on in and share my happiness!"

'Then the servant who had been given two thousand coins came in and said, "You gave me two thousand coins, sir. Look! Here are another two thousand that I have earned." "Well done, you good and faithful servant!" said his master. "You have been faithful in managing small amounts, so I will put you in charge of large amounts. Come on in and share my happiness!"

'Then the servant who had received one thousand coins came in and said, "Sir, I know you are a hard man; you reap harvests where you did not sow, and you gather crops where you did not scatter seed. I was afraid, so I went off and hid your money in the ground. Look! Here is what belongs to you."

'"You bad and lazy servant!" his master said. "You knew, did you not that I reap harvests where I did not sow, and gather crops where I did not scatter seed? Well, then, you should have deposited my money in the bank, and I would have received it all back with interest when I returned. Now, take the money away from him and give it to the one who has ten thousand coins."'

🎵 'The wise may bring their learning' (*BBC Complete Come and Praise* 64)

Lord God,
Thank you for making us all so different.
Some of us are tall and some small.
Some have blue eyes, and some brown hair.
We thank you for our different experiences,
    and for our likes and dislikes.
Help us to accept the way in which we are made.
Help us to be thankful that you made each one of us so special.
    Amen.

→ *RE*
Following on from the investigation in assembly, allow the pupils to gather oval stones that would fit the palm of their hand. Encourage them to get to know their stone so that they could pick it out from any others. Then use them to make 'prayer stones'—stones that are painted in silence and then used as a meditative focus for prayer.

Science
Pursue the quest for diversity by going on a 'mini-hike'. Allocate to pairs of pupils a measured section of ground, to conduct a survey of the different plants and animals found.

IT
Record the results of the 'mini-hike' on a prepared data base.

Different abilities (class assembly)

Today's assembly looks further at the different abilities God gives to each person.

Look at one of the following with the class:

- Pictures showing the different artwork of a number of famous artists.

- The talents of three or four pupils. Encourage them to demonstrate their talents (e.g., play a musical instrument, talk about a hobby).

We cannot all do the same things. We have different abilities. Some people are good at playing an instrument or singing, others are good at playing sport or at making others happy. Everyone has some special ability.

God gave us many different abilities (or 'gifts' as they are called in the New Testament), to be used to help each other. Our world needs all these gifts, so that we can train doctors, parents, scientists, and athletes.

In the New Testament St Paul speaks of the special gifts that are given to a church, in this case at Corinth. He calls these 'spiritual gifts'. 1 Corinthians 12.1, 4–7:

Now, concerning what you wrote about the gifts from the Holy Spirit. I want you to know the truth about them, my brothers . . .

There are different kinds of spiritual gifts, but the same Spirit gives them. There are different ways of serving, but the same Lord is served. There are different abilities to perform service, but the same God gives ability to all for their particular service. The Spirit's presence is shown in some way in each person for the good of all.

Give each person in the class a piece of paper and a pencil. Then ask them to think of one thing which they are good at and, in silence, to draw themselves doing it. As they draw, encourage them to say a silent 'Thank you' to God for their gift. Conclude with this prayer.

Lord God,
You gave us different gifts and different abilities.
Help us to use them to make this world
    a better place in which to live.   Amen.

English
Further explore differences by conducting a survey of the children's families; for example, what work do different members do within the home. Use the information to discuss issues concerning gender and role.

RE
Following the reading of Paul's letter to the Corinthians, invite visitors into school from a local church to talk about the work they do for the church; for example, the organist, the vicar or minister, a flower arranger. Alternatively, create a display showing *all* those who are involved in working for a local church.

The odd one out (school assembly)

This assembly looks at the way we sometimes discriminate against each other because of our differences, and remembers that Jesus used such an example to tell the greatest story of all time.

Tell the stories of the 'low and high heels' and the 'Big-Endians' as told in *Gulliver's Travels* by Jonathan Swift (Part 1: Chapter 4). This could be accompanied by pupils dressed in appropriate costume.

Sometimes we turn against people because they don't look like us, or because they wear different clothes. Sometimes the reason is even sillier, as we have just seen. Unfortunately, things like this have caused hurt to people, or even wars before now. We must always be careful not to make people feel the odd ones out.

At the time of Jesus, the Jews hated the Samaritans, even more perhaps than they hated the Romans who had conquered them, because the Samaritans had built a temple of their own. The Jews believed there should only be one Temple—in Jerusalem.

Our reading today is about a Samaritan. The Jews must certainly have disliked this story by Jesus because it is about a good Samaritan, and as far as they were concerned there could be no such person as a *good* Samaritan—they were all evil! Luke 10.30–35:

'There was once a man who was going down from Jerusalem to Jericho when robbers attacked him, stripped him, and beat him up, leaving him half dead. It so happened that a priest was going down that road; but when he saw the man, he walked on by, on the other side. In the same way a Levite also came along, went over and looked at the man, and then walked on by, on the other side. But a Samaritan who was travelling that way came upon the man, and when he saw him, his heart was filled with pity. He went over to him, poured oil and wine on his wounds and bandaged them; then he put the man on his own animal and took him to an inn, where he took care of him. The next day he took out two silver coins and gave them to the innkeeper. "Take care of him," he told the innkeeper, "and when I come back this way, I will pay you whatever else you spend on him."'

 'I was lying in the roadway' (*BBC Complete Come and Praise* 88)

Lord God,
Sometimes we disagree with each other,
   and argue over unimportant things.
Help us to think before we speak,
   and to be sensitive to those who
   feel they are the odd ones out.   Amen.

RE
Follow up the idea of 'the odd one out' by telling the Old Testament story of Ruth. Then talk about how she might have felt in a strange country far from home. Who made her feel welcome? Look at how new children are made welcome in the school, and think about allocating 'Parents' to them to help them settle in.

English
Create some role-play based on an irrational (and silly) prejudice (e.g., all those with brown hair). Make sure that everyone understands that it is role-play and not for real, then divide the class into the two groups. Make life difficult for those with brown hair (e.g., keep them working, make them run round, and don't let them talk). Be much softer on the other group. Afterwards discuss how each group felt.

Art

Using a sketch-book, collect visual evidence to create a picture on the theme of 'The odd one out'. Include inanimate objects and animals.

Science

Continuing the theme of the assembly, present pupils with a number of different materials (e.g., different rocks and soils, or materials distinguished by properties such as strength or flexibility). Encourage them to sort the materials into groups.

Living with our differences (class assembly)

In accepting other people's differences it is important to accept ourselves. We can change our behaviour but not our bodies. Accepting ourselves as God accepts us is a major step forward in life.

Ask the class to work in pairs, telling each other their 'body' history. What scars, broken bones, operations, or illnesses have they undergone and when? This could be translated into a chart:

Hannah Jones

1990	Broke arm
1992	Had flu badly
1993	Sprained ankle
1994	Ear infection

Discuss which parts of their body each child feels *good* about.

Physically we look very different from one another. Perhaps we take after parents or grandparents. Often we have inherited certain characteristics from them: our height, the colour of our hair, the size of our hands, or the shape of our chin. Sometimes we also inherit illnesses like diabetes or sickle-cell anaemia.

As well as looking very different from one another, our bodies also have different histories. Some of us have had broken bones, operations, or hurt ourselves in other ways. Some of us, of course, have been lucky and not damaged ourselves.

Most of us are not completely happy with the way we have been made. Perhaps we wish we had different colour hair, or that it was straight (or curly!). Jesus understood what it was like to feel like this. He spent much of his life healing people; not just healing their bodies, but the way they thought.

In this reading from the New Testament Jesus understood how Zacchaeus felt. He was *a very small man* who was hated by his fellow Jews because he collected the taxes for the Roman Empire. Notice that Jesus specially chose him from the crowd, despite the fact that a good Jew was forbidden from having anything to do with a man like Zacchaeus. Luke 19.1–10.

Jesus went on into Jericho and was passing through. There was a chief tax collector there named Zacchaeus, who was rich. He was trying to see who Jesus was, but he was a little man and could not see Jesus because of the crowd. So he ran ahead of the crowd and climbed a sycamore tree to see Jesus, who was going to pass that way. When Jesus came to that place, he looked up and said to Zacchaeus, 'Hurry down, Zacchaeus, because I must stay in your house today.'

Zacchaeus hurried down and welcomed him with great joy. All the people who saw it started grumbling, 'This man has gone as a guest to the home of a sinner!'

Zacchaeus stood up and said to the Lord, 'Listen, sir! I will give half my belongings to the poor, and if I have cheated anyone, I will pay him back four times as much.'

Jesus said to him, 'Salvation has come to this house today, for this man, also, is a descendant of Abraham. The Son of Man came to seek and to save the lost.'

Lord God,
You made each of us very different from one another,
    help us to accept ourselves as we are.
Teach us to be aware when people are unhappy
    about the way they look.
Show us how to make them feel better
    as Jesus showed Zacchaeus.   Amen.

Science
If pupils have been investigating the differences between them as a result of this week's assembly theme, continue by measuring the height of each child. Display the different heights on a wall chart. Or draw round hands, or measure span or length of fingers. Display the results.

English
Follow up the assembly by looking at disability. Discuss what it might feel like if you were an adult who was 0.8m or 2.3m tall? What might it be like to live in a house with normal-sized doors/ cupboards and beds etc.? Alternatively, create passports for each child, describing their features exactly.

IT
If statistics have been collected on the pupils as part of Science, enter these onto a prepared data base.

Maths
Use a study of number patterns to highlight *differences*, or compare objects and events measuring them with non-standard units of length or mass, and again highlight differences.

RE
Look at other stories about outcasts; for example, Jesus heals a boy with an evil spirit (Luke 9.37–43), or the ten lepers (Luke 17.11–19).

Different products (school assembly)

This assembly looks at the idea that sometimes people are not what they seem. Our differences mean that only by our behaviour will we be known.

Take some products, and cover up their real names. Make up brand names for each product. Each item should be as similar as possible to its 'twin'. For example:

- 2 different boxes of soap powder
- 2 different bars of soap
- 2 different balls.

Create some suitable advertising. For example:

Soap powder A: Brand A will wash clothes whiter than white! Try the iron test—Brand A doesn't leave a lingering smell on your clothes. Guaranteed to wash your clothes as new.

Soap powder B: Brand B will wash your clothes whiter than any other washing powder. It removes grease stains at low temperatures, and leaves clothes like new.

Ensure that the advertising is similar for both products, so that it is difficult to choose between them.

Create a role-play where all the products (or only one) are advertised in a suitable salesman-like manner. Interview 'members of the public' and ask them questions like:

- Which product would you buy, A or B?
- How do you know which is the best product?
- Do you believe the advertising?
- How do you know the advertising is true?

Conclude with a final sales pitch about the product.

As we have seen over the last few assemblies, people are all different. They look and sound different from one another, and they have usually had different experiences. However, sometimes it is difficult to tell people apart, rather like these products. How do we know which washing powder is the best? The only way we know that is if we try both powders and decide which one washes our clothes cleanest. It is rather the same with people. We only know what people are really like by their behaviour.

Of course we can be just the same! We pretend that we are someone's friend or we are brave, when in fact we are not their friend or we are not brave. Only the way we act will tell other people what we are really like.

The reading today is about two people who joined the new Christian Church. Most of the people gave up all they had to help everyone else, but two people only pretended to do so. What they said and what they did did not match up. Acts 4.32—5.10:

The group of believers was one in mind and heart. No one said that any of his belongings was his own, but they all shared with one another everything they had. With great power the apostles gave witness to the resurrection of the Lord Jesus, and God poured rich blessings on them all. There was no one in the group who was in need. Those who owned fields or houses would sell them, bring the money received from the sale, and hand it over to the apostles; and the money was distributed to each one according to his need.

And so it was that Joseph, a Levite born in Cyprus, whom the apostles called Barnabas (which means 'One who Encourages'), sold a field he owned, brought the money, and handed it over to the apostles.

But there was a man named Ananias, who with his wife Sapphira sold some property that belonged to them. But with his wife's agreement he kept part of the money for himself and handed the rest over to the apostles. Peter said to him, 'Ananias, why did you let Satan take control of you and make you lie to the Holy Spirit by keeping part of the money you received for the property? Before you sold the property, it belonged to you; and after you sold it, the money was yours. Why, then, did you decide to do such a thing? You have not lied to men—you have lied to God!'

 ''Spirit of God' (*BBC Complete Come and Praise* 85)

Lord God,
Sometimes we are not what we seem;
   we say one thing but act in another way.
Help us to speak and act in the same way,
   so that the good things said of us are true.   Amen.

RE
Follow up the thinking about words and behaviour in the assembly by reading another story about deception: the woman at the well (John 4. 1–18).

English
Explore emotions and feelings which may affect our behaviour, and which we may try to hide: anger, jealousy, fear, shyness. Talk about how we feel and about how we pretend otherwise. Read stories that reflect some of these (e.g., Jill Tomlinson, *The Owl who was Afraid of the Dark*; Ezra Jack Keats, *Peter's Chair*; Brian Sibley, *The Frightful Food Feud*).

Art
Look at emotions, by painting pictures that represent how pupils

feel when they are angry, happy, or jealous. For example, what colour, texture, and shapes will they use? Review and display.

PE
Link the assembly, and other curricular areas, to dance by encouraging pupils to create dance to reflect different emotions.

Week 5

POWER

This assembly theme looks at power: at the power of the weather and its destructive force whether caused by rain, frost, snow, or wind; and at the power of God as ultimately stronger than anything on earth.

God's great power (school assembly)

God's power is greater than any power of nature, yet despite his power he is gentle with us.

Before the assembly starts, hang some 'wind chimes' over a door or from the ceiling where they will move. These could have been made by pupils. Encourage pupils and staff to enter in silence. When all have entered, listen to some music played by wind instruments, or play a tape of Mendelssohn's *Fingal's Cave* Overture.

Speak about the power of the wind—trees blown over, roofs blown off—and of hurricanes and typhoons. Slides could be used to show the effect of the wind. Comment that the wind is one of the most powerful forces on earth.

Many years ago there was a man called Elijah. He was a prophet and because he spoke up so loudly for God, the queen grew angry and attempted to have him killed. He was forced to flee and hide in a cave.

While he was hiding in the cave, God came to him and proved that God is more powerful than anyone on earth. But if God was more powerful than the strongest wind, his power was also gentle, as we shall hear in our Bible story.

Elijah and the power of God. 1 Kings 19.8–16.

Elijah got up, ate and drank, and the food gave him enough strength to walk forty days to Sinai, the holy mountain. There he went into a cave to spend the night.

Suddenly the Lord spoke to him, 'Elijah, what are you doing here?'

He answered, 'Lord God Almighty, I have always served you—you alone. But the people of Israel have broken their covenant with you, torn down your altars, and killed all your prophets. I am the only one left—and they are trying to kill me!'

'Go out and stand before me on top of the mountain,' the Lord said to him. Then the Lord passed by and sent a furious wind that split the hills and shattered the rocks—but the Lord was not in the wind. The wind stopped blowing, and then there was an earthquake—but the Lord was not in the earthquake. After the earthquake, there was a fire—but the Lord was not in the fire. And after the fire, there was the soft whisper of a voice.

When Elijah heard it, he covered his face with his cloak and went out and stood at the entrance of the cave.

'A still small voice' (*BBC Complete Come and Praise* 96)

_____

Before the assembly, prepare a 'wind dance' with a group of pupils. Explore the different moods of the wind, and its effect upon humans, using contrasting speed and shape (e.g., cold and windy day, or a sunny and blustery one, or a still day). Accompany the dance with music if desired.

_____

Lord God,
We see the power of the wind,
   how it blows down trees and houses,
   how it stirs the sea to great strength.
We know that you are more powerful than all this
   for you have made everything that exists
Yet you love us as a parent loves a child,
   so we ask that you deal gently with us this day.   Amen.

Music
Follow up the work on wind by using tuned and untuned instruments, as well as the voice, to create a piece of music titled 'The wayward wind'.

Design and Technology
Take up the idea from the assembly to initiate a project on the wind. Design a way of collecting information on wind speed. Produce a prototype, test and adjust it, before making the finished version. Gather information over the period of a week.

IT
Organize and present the information gathered on the wind in a number of ways, and store the information in a retrieval system.

Geography
Continue the work on wind by finding out more about wind speeds, hurricanes, tornadoes, and cloud formations.

RE
God appeared to Elijah as a whisper. Investigate other images of God (e.g., in the Psalms) as shepherd, king, warrior etc.

PE
Create some dance based on the different moods of the wind and its effect on humans. Use contrasting speed and shape, and accompany with music.

Strength in weakness (school or class assembly)

Many people feel that they are too weak and small to make any major changes to the world. This assembly explores how individuals, with God's help, have the power to make a difference.

Talk about times when pupils might feel helpless: when they are faced with pictures of starving children on TV, when they hear about natural disasters, or experience situations beyond their control at home or at school.

Often we feel we cannot change a situation because we are only one small person. However, we should not feel like this. Whatever the situation, we can make a difference. Sometimes we can change things by working together with others who might feel the same. Then instead of being a person alone we become many—and this can make a big difference.

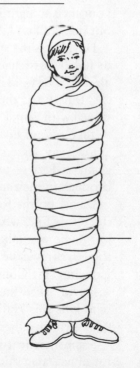

Take a toilet roll and tear off one sheet. Ask for a volunteer to tear the paper in half (they will obviously achieve this easily). Then ask if they think they will always be able to tear toilet paper apart so easily? (They will probably answer Yes!) Proceed to demonstrate that this is not always true, by wrapping the child up like a mummy using the whole roll of paper, and ensuring you go over and over the same part. The child should now find it very difficult to tear the toilet paper—if not impossible.

Comment that one sheet of paper is easy to tear—it is fairly weak—but a large number of sheets can be very much more difficult. When we are alone we can do little to change any situation, but together, and especially with God's help, we can make a big difference.

🎵 (For school assembly.)
'Father, hear the prayer we offer' (BBC *Complete Come and Praise* 48)

📖 The Bible teaches us that we can always make a difference. One person, with God's help, can change a world, as we see from today's reading. From 1 Samuel 17:

The Philistines gathered for battle in Socoh, a town in Judah . . .

A man named Goliath, from the city of Gath, came out from the Philistine camp to challenge the Israelites. He was nearly three metres tall and wore bronze armour that weighed about fifty-seven kilograms and a bronze helmet. His legs were also protected by bronze armour, and he carried a bronze javelin slung over his shoulder. His spear was as thick as the bar on a weaver's loom, and its iron head weighed about seven kilograms. A soldier walked in front of him carrying his shield. Goliath stood and shouted at the Israelites, 'What are you doing there, lined up for battle? I am a Philistine, you slaves of Saul! Choose one of your men to fight me. If he wins and kills me, we will be your slaves; but if I win and kill him, you will be our slaves . . .'

David was the son of Jesse, who was an Ephrathite from Bethlehem in Judah. Jesse had eight sons, and at the time Saul was king, he was already a very old man. His three eldest sons had gone with Saul to war . . . David was the youngest son, and while the three eldest brothers stayed with Saul, David would go back to Bethlehem from time to time, to take care of his father's sheep . . .

One day Jesse said to David, 'Take ten kilograms of this roasted grain and these ten loaves of bread, and hurry with them to your brothers in the camp . . .'

David left the food with the officer in charge of the supplies, ran to the battle line, went to his brothers and asked how they were getting on. As he was talking to them, Goliath came forward and challenged the Israelites as he had done before. And David heard him. When the Israelites saw Goliath, they ran away in terror . . .

David asked the men who were near him, 'What will the man get who kills this Philistine and frees Israel from this disgrace? After all, who is this heathen Philistine to defy the army of the living God?' . . .

Some men heard what David had said, and they told Saul, who sent for him. David said to Saul, 'Your Majesty, no one should be afraid of this Philistine! I will go and fight him.'

'No,' answered Saul. 'How could you fight him? You're just a boy, and he has been a soldier all his life!'

'Your Majesty,' David said, 'I take care of my father's sheep. Whenever a lion or a bear carries off a lamb, I go after it, attack it, and rescue the lamb. And if the lion or bear turns on me, I grab it by the throat and beat it to death. I have killed lions and bears, and I will do the same to this heathen Philistine, who has defied the army of the living God. The Lord has saved me from lions and bears; he will save me from this Philistine.'

'All right,' Saul answered. 'Go, and the Lord be with you.' . . . David took his shepherd's stick and then picked up five smooth stones from the stream and put them in his bag. With his catapult ready, he went out to meet Goliath.

The Philistine started walking towards David, with his shield-bearer walking in front of him. He kept coming closer, and when he got a good look at David, he was filled with scorn for him because he was just a nice, good-looking boy. He said to David, 'What's that stick for? Do you think I'm a dog?' . . .

David answered, 'You are coming against me with sword, spear, and javelin, but I come against you in the name of the Lord God Almighty, the God of the Israelite armies, which you have defied.' . . .

Goliath started walking towards David again, and David ran quickly towards the Philistine battle line to fight him. He put his hand into his bag and took out a stone, which he slung at Goliath. It hit him on the forehead and broke his skull, and Goliath fell face downwards on the ground . . . When the Philistines saw that their hero was dead, they ran away.

Lord God,
We pray for those who are small or weak:
    for children who are frightened,
    for animals in danger,
    for old people who live alone.
We pray for children who have no food and no homes,
    and for those caught up in the middle of disaster or war.
Help us to work together to change our world
    so that it may be a better place for us all to live.   Amen.

61

RE
Look at other examples of weakness overcoming strength in the Bible: for example, Daniel's three friends thrown into the fire (Daniel 3.8–30); Daniel in the lion's den (Daniel 6.1–28).

Science
Look at the idea of size and strength, and experiment with seeds. Discover if seed size determines the ultimate size of the plant.

Music
Look at size in music: for example, listen to Benjamin Britten's *Young Person's Guide to the Orchestra* and find out more about the piccolo and the double bass. How large are these instruments? Do noise and size equate?

English
David had no fear, even though he was to fight a giant. Read *The Very Worried Sparrow* by Meryl Doney and talk about overcoming fears.

Power of the Son (school assembly)

This assembly looks at God's power as seen in the life of Jesus and reminds us that this power is still at work in the world today.

 Before the assembly, gather together the following items and place on a table:

- 1 white handkerchief
- 1 glass half-filled with water
- a small bottle of Iodine
- 1 glass half-filled with water *and* 2 spoons of sodium thiosulphate in crystal form (available from any chemist).

At the start of the assembly, tell the pupils that you want to show them something amazing.

When you are ready, pour a good quantity of iodine onto a white handkerchief. Show the pupils the resulting yellow mark, and ask them if they think it will become clean if you put it in water. Then put the handkerchief into the glass full of water. The stain will turn dark grey or black. Indicate horror!

Suggest that you know you can get the handkerchief perfectly clean by dipping it into the other glass of water. (The pupils may express disbelief.)

Finally, put the handkerchief into the glass containing the sodium thiosulphate. The handkerchief will instantly become clean, to the amazement of everyone.

There is an explanation for this amazing happening (tell them what you have put into the water). Why the sodium thiosulphate acts on the iodine as it does is difficult to understand.

The theme for today's assembly is the power of Jesus—a power which we believe is still available today. When Jesus carried out his miracles, people must have been as amazed as we have been about the iodine disappearing. How did he make the lame walk, the blind see, and the deaf hear?

We do not know how the miracles of Jesus happened. We still have no explanations, although we might guess at some of the answers. What we do know is that he had the power to do many things that were truly amazing, and later the disciples were also given this same power. They healed the sick—often people who had been unable to walk for many years—and brought the dead to life. There are many stories of the extraordinary things that happened in the letters and writings of the new Church.

But that is not the end of the story, for Christians believe that God still carries out miracles today. Sometimes people are healed in ways that no one can really explain—perhaps after church members have prayed with them. The amazing things haven't stopped happening, though they do not always happen just because we pray for God's help. God does not always answer our prayers just as we would like, though that should not stop us asking him to help.

In this reading Jesus heals Bartimaeus who is blind, because he has faith that Jesus can heal him. Mark 10.46–52:

They came to Jericho, and as Jesus was leaving with his disciples and a large crowd, a blind beggar named Bartimaeus son of Timaeus was sitting by the road. When he heard that it was Jesus of Nazareth, he began to shout, 'Jesus! Son of David! Take pity on me!'

Many of the people scolded him and told him to be quiet. But he shouted even more loudly, 'Son of David, take pity on me!'

Jesus stopped and said, 'Call him.' So they called the blind man. 'Cheer up!' they said. 'Get up, he is calling you.'

He threw off his cloak, jumped up, and came to Jesus.

'What do you want me to do for you?' Jesus asked him.

'Teacher,' the blind man answered, 'I want to see again.'

'Go,' Jesus told him, 'your faith has made you well.'

At once he was able to see and followed Jesus on the road.

'Go tell it on the mountain' (*BBC Complete Come and Praise* 24)

Light one or more candles. Ask pupils to focus on them and to think about anyone they know who is ill; this might be an individual, or those suffering in a particular part of the world. Use the following litany:

Leader: Hear us as we pray for those who are ill.
(*Silence*)

Leader: Lord, hear our prayer.
All: And let our cry come unto you.

Leader: Hear us as we pray for those who are frightened.
(*Silence*)

Leader: Lord, hear our prayer.
  All: And let our cry come unto you.

Leader: Hear us as we pray for those who are suffering.
(*Silence*)

Leader: Lord, hear our prayer.
  All: And let our cry come unto you.

Or, use this prayer:

> Lord God,
> We read about the miracles performed by Jesus
>   when he healed the sick and the suffering.
> Help us to know that you still perform miracles
>   as we remember those who are sick today
>   and ask for your healing power to be with them.
> Amen.

➡️ *RE*
Follow up the story of Bartimaeus by reading other stories about miracles: for example, the feeding of the five thousand (Mark 6.34–44); Jesus walks on water (Mark 6.45–52); the deaf mute (Mark 7.31–37). Read any modern story about a healing. Make a list of those who are sick in school and pray for them (perhaps in silence) at assemblies this week.

History
Continue the theme of power by looking at the role of the monarchy and at the theory of the divine right of kings if the class are studying life in Tudor times. Examine the custom of Maundy money and the washing of feet by the monarch.

English
Rewrite a miracle story using simple phrases. Put the phrases onto pieces of thin card. Encourage pupils to work in groups and to piece the story together correctly. For example:

Lots of people   They became
went with Jesus.   hungry.

Jesus took
five loaves and
two fish
and gave thanks
to God.

All the people
had the food and
there was still some
left.

(Taken from the feeding of the five thousand.)

Plugged into power (school assembly)

This assembly reminds us that we must keep in regular touch with God through prayer.

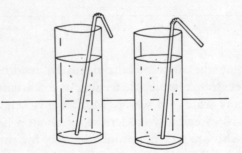

Before the assembly, purchase two or three small bottles or cans of fizzy drink. Place straws in the drinks, and make sure that one or two of the straws are pierced with a needle, leaving a small hole, so that they cannot work effectively.

Ask for volunteers to help. Give each of them a bottle or can and ask them to drink from it *without taking the straw out of the container*. Let each child try for a moment before asking those who cannot get anything out what is the matter. Ask them to try again—they can't be trying hard enough!

Finally, have a look at the straws and establish that there is a hole so nothing will come out. Then allow the pupils to finish the drink if they wish, replacing the straws with new ones.

This week we have been looking at the theme of power. We have looked at the power of God as seen in the Old Testament, and we have seen the power that Jesus used to work miracles. But one question we have not asked is: 'If God is so powerful why don't miracles happen more often today?'

Perhaps the experiment with the drinks helps to show us the problem. It is impossible to drink from a straw when there is a hole. In the same way it is very difficult for us to communicate with God if there is a problem with our channel of communication.

Very often we only speak to God when there is an emergency, so the communication channel gets blocked up and unusable (rather like the straws!). Speaking to God should be like talking to a friend who always listens, but who does not always let us have our own way. Just because we ask for something doesn't mean we will always get it.

In our reading, St Luke says we should continually speak to God— ask him, knock at his door, and look for him wherever we go. Luke 11.9–13:

'And so I say to you: Ask, and you will receive; seek, and you will find; knock, and the door will be opened to you. For everyone who asks will receive, and he who seeks will find, and the door will be opened to anyone who knocks. Would any of you who are fathers give your son a snake when he asks for fish? Or would you give him a scorpion when he asks for an egg? Bad as you are, you know how to give good things to your children. How much more, then, will the Father in heaven give the Holy Spirit to those who ask him!'

 Create biddings (e.g., Lord God, we pray for all children . . .) asking different pupils to read them, then sing the Taizé chorus 'O Lord hear my prayer' after each bidding prayer.

'Seek ye first' (*Mission Praise* 201)

RE
Pick up the idea of prayer from the assembly by discussing different styles of prayer (intercession, petition, confession, praise etc.). Create prayers in these styles for use in future assemblies.

History
If the class are working on the study unit Romans, Anglo-Saxons and Vikings in Britain, look at the religious life of the early monasteries: number of services in a day, different jobs within the monastery, clothing, etc. Or look at worship from Roman times to the present day. This could be centred on an abbey or cathedral.

PE
Use the words 'seek', 'knock', 'ask' from the music used in assembly to prepare an improvised dance.

Our power (class assembly)

Each of us has power which can be used for good or for ill. Even Jesus himself was tempted to use power in the wrong way.

Place an object in the room for pupils to focus on—perhaps a flower, or a picture. Then ask each pupil to think silently of one or two occasions when they have hurt someone or destroyed something. You might wish to give examples:

- deliberately broken something (e.g., a cup, or a moth);
- hurt another person (e.g., by saying something unkind, or by hitting them).

Finally, break the silence by saying that each one of us has *power*. We can use our arms and legs, and our brains, to do many things. We have the power to love and to hate; to care tenderly for a baby, or to hit someone!

Throughout our lives we have to make constant choices about how to use this power. One way to help us make good choices is to remember the colours of the traffic light (you might wish to produce a large picture of a traffic light):

All too often we do not stop and think before we act. If we stopped and thought we might decide to use our power in a better way.

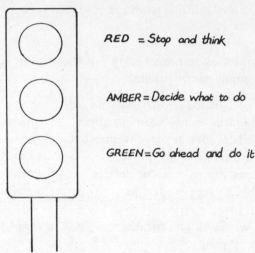

RED = Stop and think

AMBER = Decide what to do

GREEN = Go ahead and do it

Jesus was tempted to use his power in the wrong way. Luke 4.1–13:

Jesus returned from the Jordan full of the Holy Spirit and was led by the Spirit into the desert, where he was tempted by the Devil for forty days. In all that time he ate nothing, so that he was hungry when it was over.

The Devil said to him, 'If you are God's Son, order this stone to turn into bread.'

But Jesus answered, 'The scripture says, "Man cannot live on bread alone."'

Then the Devil took him up and showed him in a second all the kingdoms of the world. 'I will give you all this power and all this wealth,' the Devil told him. 'It has all been handed over to me, and I can give it to anyone I choose. All this will be yours, then, if you worship me.'

Jesus answered, 'The scripture says, "Worship the Lord your God and serve only him!"'

Then the Devil took him to Jerusalem and set him on the highest point of the Temple, and said to him, 'If you are God's Son, throw yourself down from here. For the scripture says, 'God will order his angels to take good care of you.' It also says, "They will hold you up with their hands so that not even your feet will be hurt on the stones."'

But Jesus answered, 'The scripture says, "Do not put the Lord your God to the test."'

When the Devil finished tempting Jesus in every way, he left him for a while.

During the closing prayer carry out these hand actions, encouraging the pupils to copy them.

Lord God,   (*hands slightly out and up*)
You gave us faces, not to scowl in anger,   (*grimace*)
    but to smile in love at those we meet this day.   (*smile*)
You gave us hands and the power   (*look at hands*)
    to use them, not to crush or destroy   (*fists clenched to fight*)
in hate, but to support and to   (*nursing a baby position*)
    cherish in love.
Lord God, we thank you for our   (*look at hands*)
    hands.   Amen.

RE
Follow up on the story of the temptations used in the assembly, and explore why these might have been misuses of Jesus' power. Look at what might be misuse of our power.

Science
Continue the theme of power by looking at the safety aspects of working with different materials and at the power of materials to hurt us.

Music
Using tuned or untuned instruments, create some music on the theme of power (e.g., a thunderstorm, or a storm at sea). Listen to 'Mars' from Holst's *The Planets*.

History
Look at the power of authority as part of the study unit on Romans, Anglo-Saxons and Vikings, if appropriate, and at resistance to this authority (e.g., look at Boudicca or King Alfred).

SYMBOLS

Symbols exist everywhere in our lives. They usually point beyond themselves to something of importance. For instance, we may bend over to pull up our socks or tie a shoelace, but when we bow or curtsy to another person we indicate the respect that we have for that person. The assemblies this week look particularly at symbolism in the Church.

Symbolic names (school assembly)

This assembly looks at symbolism, and in particular at the symbolism of Christian names.

In this week's assemblies we are going to look at symbols. A symbol always tells us something. It might not have any words, indeed it is usually a picture, an object or an action, but it always tells us something. For instance, these are symbols. Can you tell me what they mean? (As the actions are mimed, ask *why* you are doing these actions and *what* they mean.)

- Hand raised in the air (as in a child wanting to tell the teacher something).
- Curtsy or bow (as to a member of the Royal Family).
- Clapping (as at a performance).

There are symbols everywhere we go. Road signs are symbols. They tell us something—that there is a hospital or school nearby, or a roundabout ahead. When you leave school today have a look for two road signs near the school. See if you can find out what they mean.

The Church also uses many symbols. A common symbol is that of a name. Names can mean many things, and from earliest times first names in particular have been important. In the Old Testament we read of children who were often given names with special meanings; even today many of us have names with Christian meanings.

Prior to the assembly, arrange for some pupils to read out the definition of their names. Any dictionary of names will give you a wide selection. Here are a few suggestions.

First names from the Old or New Testament

Sarah   From the Hebrew (i.e. Jewish) meaning 'Princess'.

Michael From the Hebrew, meaning 'who is like God'.

John   From the Hebrew, meaning 'the Lord is gracious'. A favourite name in the Eastern Church, which was brought into England via the Crusaders.

Jesus gave Simon, one of his disciples, a symbolic name which meant 'rock', for he was to be the rock on which he built his Church. Matthew 16.13–19:

Jesus went to the territory near the town of Caesarea Philippi, where he asked his disciples, 'Who do people say the Son of Man is?'

'Some say John the Baptist,' they answered. 'Others say Elijah, while others say Jeremiah or some other prophet.'

'What about you?' he asked them. 'Who do you say I am?'

Simon Peter answered, 'You are the Messiah, the Son of the living God.'

'Good for you, Simon son of John!' answered Jesus. 'For this truth did not come to you from any human being, but it was given to you directly by my Father in heaven. And so I call you, Peter: you are a rock, and on this rock foundation I will build my church, and not even death will ever be able to overcome it. I will give you the keys of the Kingdom of heaven; what you prohibit on earth will be prohibited in heaven, and what you permit on earth will be permitted in heaven.'

'Every word comes alive' (*BBC Complete Come and Praise* 72)

 Use an over-head projector if possible to display pictures for 'eyes-open' prayer.

Lord God,
We thank you for our world and for all those things we use as symbols:

for our names   [put up a picture showing many names written all
                  over the page in any direction]

              (*Pause*)

for our actions   [put up a picture of people waving, bowing, curtsy-
                  ing and clapping]

              (*Pause*)

for the cross   [put up a picture of different crosses]

              (*Pause*)

We thank you for all that symbols mean to us.   Amen.

RE
Continue researching the names of pupils started in the assembly, looking at family origins, saints' names etc. Look up the following Bible readings, where people were named for a purpose: Exodus 2.22; 1 Samuel 1.20; Hosea 1.2–9.

English
Plan and draft a story for a much younger child about someone whose behaviour matches the meaning of their name.

IT
Record the stories to use with younger children, and evaluate.

Geography
Follow up the idea of symbols and road signs in the assembly by looking at local maps and identifying a range of symbols.

Mathematics
Compare objects using non-standard units of measurement and allow pupils to create their own symbols for these.

The fish (school or class assembly)

One of the oldest symbols in Christianity is the fish. This assembly looks at its meaning and use in the Bible, and remembers that it was used by those suffering persecution.

Cut out some fish shapes from newspapers. The fish can be of various shapes but should be of similar size (approximately 50 cm long).

Ask for some volunteers, and give each pupil one of the paper fishes and a piece of card. Then run a 'fish race'—by flapping the card behind the fish so that the draught moves the fish along the floor. Anyone who actually touches the fish has to start again!

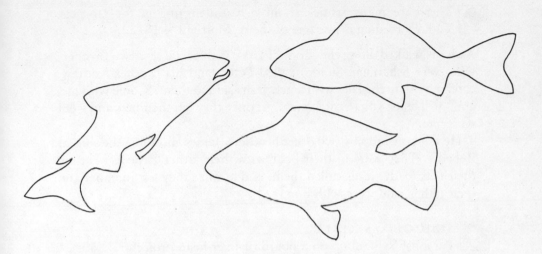

This week we are thinking about symbols, that is, pictures, actions, or objects that tell us of something else. Today we are looking at the fish, one of the most famous Christian symbols. Perhaps you have seen Christians wearing badges showing a fish symbol, or seen fish symbols in the backs of cars. But why a fish?

Well, in the early days of the Christian Church, when Christians were being persecuted for their faith, it was safer not to speak to others in case you were caught by the Romans. So symbols were used to identify people. The fish was used because each letter of the Greek word for fish is the first letter of each of the words Jesus Christ, God's Son, Saviour, and probably also because many of the Apostles were fishermen. Jesus also asked his disciples to come and 'catch men'. Someone coming across the outline of a fish drawn on the wall of the caves under the city of Rome, for instance, would draw in the eyes of the fish, as a sign that they recognized the symbol.

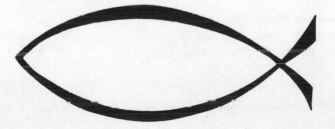

Jesus Christ
God's Son
Saviour

There are many stories about fish and fishing in the Gospels. Today's reading is just one of them. Matthew 4.18–22:

As Jesus walked along the shore of Lake Galilee, he saw two brothers who were fishermen, Simon (called Peter) and his brother Andrew, catching fish in the lake with a net. Jesus said to them, 'Come with me, and I will teach you to catch men.' At once they left their nets and went with him.

He went on and saw two other brothers, James and John, the sons of Zebedee. They were in their boat with their father Zebedee, getting their nets ready. Jesus called them, and at once they left the boat and their father, and went with him.

SCHOOL.ASSEMBLY
Put a fish symbol up on a board or over-head projector.

Lord God,
We pray for all Christians
    and especially for those in this parish.
We thank you that we are free to worship
    and pray for those who are persecuted for their faith.   Amen.

'I danced in the morning' (BBC *Complete Come and Praise* 22)

CLASS ASSEMBLY
Give each pupil a piece of paper and ask them to draw an outline of a fish and to mark in the eyes. Then spend a moment in silence praying for all Christians, and especially for those who live and worship in local churches.

RE
Read other stories about fish and fishing from the Bible: for example, Jesus calms the storm (Matthew 8.23–27); Jesus walks on the water (Mark 6.45–52); Jesus at the lakeside (John 21.1–14).

Art
Continue this idea by creating a collage, printing, or origami based on Jesus calming the storm.

English
Listen to poems about fish: for example, 'The joy of fishes' by Chuang Tzu in *Can I Buy a Slice of the Sky* (ed. Grace Nichols).

The cross (class assembly)

This assembly looks at the symbol of the cross. The cross has always been one of the most important of symbols for Christians.

The cross was not the first symbol to be used by Christians (the fish was probably the first), but it soon became the most important symbol.

Crucifixion was a common form of death in Roman times for those who went against the state, and Jesus was crucified despite being innocent of any crime against the Roman Empire. We remember his death by placing crosses in church, hanging them round our necks, putting them on Bibles, and even physically making the sign of the cross.

There are many different kinds of crosses. A cross that comes from the British Isles is the Celtic cross. It has a circle around it to show that God is always with us—because a circle has no end.

Draw Celtic crosses and fill them with Celtic designs, or make a Celtic border around them (i.e., use interlacing patterns with pictures of animals interwoven).

The story of Jesus and Thomas. This is the story of a man who found it difficult to believe that Jesus had actually died on the cross and risen again. John 20.24–29:

One of the twelve disciples, Thomas (called the Twin), was not with them when Jesus came. So the other disciples told him, 'We have seen the Lord!'

Thomas said to them, 'Unless I see the scars of the nails in his hands and put my finger on those scars and my hand in his side, I will not believe.'

A week later the disciples were together again indoors, and Thomas was with them. The doors were locked, but Jesus came and stood among them and said, 'Peace be with you.' Then he said to Thomas, 'Put your finger here, and look at my hands; then stretch out your hand and put it in my side. Stop your doubting, and believe!'

Thomas answered him, 'My Lord and my God!'

Jesus said to him, 'Do you believe because you see me? How happy are those who believe without seeing me!'

Ask each pupil to hold the picture of their Celtic cross in front of them and look at it (whether or not they are finished) and to picture the scene as the words of the prayer are read.

Lord God,
We look at this Celtic cross,
   a sign of your love for us: (*pause*)
As its upright reaches from earth to heaven,
   you draw all creatures to yourself.   (*pause*)
As its crosspiece stretches from east to west,
   your arms are spread wide to hold everybody.   (*pause*)
As the circle surrounds the cross,
   so your love surrounds us.   (*pause*)   Amen.

RE
Continue looking at crosses by investigating other cross shapes: for example, the Latin cross, the Maltese cross, the crucifix, St Andrew's cross (see W. Ellwood Post, *Saints, Signs, and Symbols*). Visit an Anglican or Roman Catholic church and hunt for crosses—how many different kinds can be found?

Music
Learn a hymn about the crucifixion (e.g., 'There is a green hill').

English
Read Brian Wildsmith, *The True Cross*, or Angela Elwell Hunt, *The Tale of Three Trees.*

Mathematics
Copy and make patterns from Celtic art using reflection and rotation.

Bread (school or class assembly)

Another symbol of importance to the Christian Church is bread. This assembly explores the spiritual meaning that Jesus gave to bread, acknowledging with gratitude our food, both spiritual and material.

Before the assembly, collect pictures of as many foods as possible, or draw pictures of a variety of foodstuffs. Alternatively write the names of different foods up on a board or over-head projector. Then ask a number of pupils and staff to tell you what kinds of food they have eaten in the last 24 hours. These might include:

fish and chips	jelly	eggs
cereals	ice cream	yoghurt
bread	sweets	fish fingers
fruit	beans	salad
pizzas	cakes	beefburgers
pasta	biscuits	chips

Comment that the amount of food eaten by all the members in the class/ school would be enough to stock a shop!

All the food we have eaten reminds us of another symbol of great importance to Christians—bread. Often the Bible uses the word 'bread' to stand for all our food. We would not be alive for very long without food, and bread was one of the commonest of foods in Palestine.
Bread is still important to us today, and many of us will have eaten

some bread for our breakfast this morning. In the past there have been times when the bakers have gone on strike, or there has been an electricity strike and so no bread could be made, and the queues of people waiting to buy it have been enormous.

Often we take bread for granted, but without it we would really miss it for breakfast, lunch and dinner. Jesus knew how much people relied on bread. He used it to explain how much they needed God. He said he was like bread—the bread of life. Just as people could not go without food for their bodies, so they could not go without food for their soul.

Jesus is the bread of life. John 6.28–35:

So [the people] asked him, 'What can we do in order to do what God wants us to do?'

Jesus answered, 'What God wants you to do is to believe in the one he sent.'

They replied, 'What miracle will you perform so that we may see it and believe you? What will you do? Our ancestors ate manna in the desert, just as the scripture says, "He gave them bread from heaven to eat."'

'I am telling you the truth,' Jesus said. 'What Moses gave you was not the bread from heaven; it is my Father who gives you the real bread from heaven. For the bread that God gives is he who comes down from heaven and gives life to the world.'

'Sir,' they asked him, 'give us this bread always.'

'I am the bread of life,' Jesus told them. 'He who comes to me will never be hungry; he who believes in me will never be thirsty.'

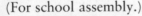 (For school assembly.)
'I saw the man from Galilee' (*BBC Complete Come and Praise* 75)

Lord God,
We thank you for our food;
    for the food we enjoy,
      as well as the food we dislike.
We thank you for our sense of smell and taste;
    we remember those who have eating problems,
      and those who have no food and are hungry.   Amen.

Note: Space could be left for the pupils to imagine each of the thoughts during the prayer.

RE
Follow up the story of manna mentioned in the assembly by reading about Moses in the desert (Exodus 16). Continue by looking at the celebration of Holy Communion with its emphasis on a meal of bread and wine. Visit a church or invite visitors in to explore further.

Design and technology
Continue, by looking at bread in Design and Technology. Find a recipe, gather the ingredients and bake some bread.

English
Talk about being hungry. What does it feel like? What kind of thing do we prefer to eat when we are hungry? What vocabulary might we use? Read about food, or starving people (for example, in *Oxfam 50*).

Science
Follow up the theme of bread by widening it to look at what kinds of food are needed to maintain a healthy body. What do the pupils really eat?

Water (school or class assembly)

The symbol of water is as important to Christians as bread. Jesus uses the idea of water in a similar way to that of bread. The assembly also reminds us to thank God for water.

Use pupils to mime the following activities, and ask what is happening:

- filling up a kettle and plugging it in.
- opening a can of pop and drinking it.
- making and throwing snowballs.

- breathing in and out.
- being given and eating a very cold ice-lolly.
- swimming.
- washing clothes by hand.

When they have all been guessed, ask what they have in common. The answer is *water*.

All living things need water. People, animals, and all plants must have water to live. Without it we would die. Indeed, our bodies are mostly made up of water.

As we have seen, we use water to wash ourselves and our clothes; we drink it (it is in almost everything we drink—fizzy drinks, tea etc.); we swim in it; we breathe it in the air; we eat frozen water (ice-lollies and ice-cubes); we even put it into mattresses for the bed sometimes.

Often we take water for granted. However, today we remember all that it means to us, and thank God for all who help to make our water clean to use.

However, for Christians, water has another importance—it is a special symbol. It stands for new life, for the washing away of all the things we have done wrong. At baptism, we talk about the person being made clean from their sins. Just as water can make our bodies clean, so it washes away our sins, and we are able to start afresh again. As a symbol, those who are baptized have water poured onto them.

Before Jesus started his work in Palestine his cousin, John, told the people to confess their sins and be baptized in the river Jordan. Matthew 3.1–6:

At that time John the Baptist came to the desert of Judaea and started preaching. 'Turn away from your sins,' he said, 'because the Kingdom of heaven is near!' John was the man the prophet Isaiah was talking about when he said,

'Someone is shouting in the desert,
"Prepare a road for the Lord;
make a straight path for him to travel!"'

John's clothes were made of camel's hair; he wore a leather belt round his waist, and his food was locusts and wild honey. People came to him from Jerusalem, from the whole province of Judaea, and from all the country near the River Jordan. They confessed their sins, and he baptized them in the Jordan.

(For school assembly.)
'Have you heard the rain drops drumming?' (*BBC Complete Come and Praise* 2)

Encourage the pupils to keep their eyes open for this prayer. Place a large glass jug full of water (or more than one) where it can be seen. As slowly as possible, pour out a glass of water before speaking.

Lord God,
We thank you for water:
    cold water to drink on a hot sunny day,
    warm water for the shower and bath,
    the water that we breathe in the air,
    and the water we use to wash our clothes.
Help us not to take water for granted,
    but to enjoy its use in our life.   Amen.

RE
As a follow-up to the work on water, investigate baptism. Visit a local church and look at any artefacts connected with baptism (e.g., the font, shell, holy water, baptistery).

Science
Explore the water cycle, with particular attention to evaporation and condensation.

English
Read about water (*Oxfam 50* has a chapter on this including pictures), talk about what it feels like to be clean or dirty and make lists of suitable words to use.

PE
Create a dance based on the enjoyment of water.

History

If the class is working on the study unit Britain since the 1930s, follow up the assembly by exploring the changes made this century with regard to water (e.g., running water in the house and the indoor toilet). Interview people who remember using an outside pump and toilets.

PATTERNS

Our world is full of patterns—things that copy one another and look the same. We find them in the decoration of buildings, on tiles and carpets, in Mathematics, History, and even in PE.

In Christianity, there is pattern in the way people have related to God over thousands of years. The assemblies this week will be looking at this relationship.

God who listens (class assembly)

This assembly reminds us that God is always a God who listens to us.

In pairs ask each pupil in turn to talk to their partner about one of the following subjects. The listener may not interrupt the speaker. At the end of it they should repeat as much as they can remember back to the speaker. Then reverse the situation.

- My dog/cat
- The best thing in my life
- The best day I ever had
- The day I went to Alton Towers (or other theme park).

Ask what it felt like to have someone really listen to you. How often does this happen? How many times do people only partially listen to you, because they are actually thinking about what they are going to say next?

Both Jews and Christians believe that God is someone who listens to people. All we have to do is to speak to him. In the Old Testament—in the Psalms in particular—we can read what the people said to God when they were happy as well as when they feared for their lives.

Years later the pattern was continued as Jesus taught his disciples how to speak to God, a God who was always willing to listen to them.

In our first reading we hear from someone who was badly in need of help speaking to God nearly three thousand years ago. In our second reading we hear St Matthew's account of Jesus teaching his disciples about God. Psalm 5.1–8:

> Listen to my words, O Lord,
>   and hear my sighs,
> Listen to my cry for help,
>   my God and king!
>
> I pray to you, O Lord;
>   you hear my voice in the morning;
> at sunrise I offer my prayer
>   and wait for your answer.
>
> You are not a God who is pleased with wrongdoing;
>   you allow no evil in your presence.
> You cannot stand the sight of proud men;
>   you hate all wicked people.
> You destroy all liars
>   and despise violent, deceitful men.
>
> But because of your great love
>   I can come into your house;
> I can worship in your holy Temple
>   and bow down to you in reverence.
> Lord, I have so many enemies!
>   Lead me to do your will;
>   make your way plain for me to follow.

Matthew 6.5–8:

'When you pray, do not be like the hypocrites! They love to stand up and pray in the houses of worship and on the street corners, so that everyone will see them. I assure you, they have already been paid in full. But when you pray, go to your room, close the door, and pray to your Father, who is unseen. And your Father, who sees what you do in private, will reward you.

'When you pray, do not use a lot of meaningless words, as the pagans do, who think that their gods will hear them because their prayers are long. Do not be like them. Your Father already knows what you need before you ask him.'

Suggest that pupils speak to God, 'in the silence of their hearts', telling him anything they want to say. Light a candle to act as a focal point, if desired, and allow two or three minutes of silence. Conclude with these words:

Lord God,
We know that you are always listening to us,
   and we ask you to hear the prayers
   that we have spoken in our hearts.   Amen.

RE
Follow up the assembly by doing some experiential RE. Encourage pupils to close their eyes, listen to everything around them for a minute or two, and then write down everything they can hear.

Mathematics
Referring to the theme for the week, 'Patterns', follow up by looking at Mathematical patterns.

Music
Listen to some orchestral music and begin to take in the patterns made by themes and instruments (hear Benjamin Britten, *The Young Person's Guide to the Orchestra*, or Serge Prokofiev, *Peter and the Wolf*).

Art
Investigate examples of art, craft and design in the school for pattern and symmetry.

God who speaks (school or class assembly)

Another pattern we see in the Bible is that both Jews and Christians worship a God who speaks to them and whose word is to be obeyed. Today, two thousand years later, this assembly *waits on God*.

 Using a number of pupils, create two short improvised sketches on the following lines:

SKETCH 1
A visitor to a town asks two people who are walking together for directions to the station. The reply is something like this:

First speaker: Go up the High Street, turn right at the T Junction, then keep going for about 300 metres, before turning left and heading towards the hospital.

Second speaker: No! No! That's all wrong! Don't go up the High Street; take the first turning on your right, then next left, and first right. You'll see it straight ahead of you.

First speaker: That'll never get you to the station. You're more likely to end up in the river . . . !

SKETCH 2
There are three girls, one of whom is asking the other two what they think about her dress.

First speaker: It's great! I love the ―― (add a comment about the dress), and the colour's great! I wish I could look as good in . . . (colour)!

Second speaker: I wouldn't be seen dead in ――. If my Mum bought me clothes like that I'd die! Where'd she get it from, a charity shop?

―――――――――――――――

This week we are looking at patterns in the Bible, and today we look at the way that God has spoken to men and women over the centuries. Christians believe that the only reliable person in their lives is God, and that God speaks in many different ways to people, if only they will stop a moment and listen. God speaks, for instance, through our conscience, through the world and through other people.

Often we get conflicting advice, as we have just heard. Someone tells us to 'do this' and another person says 'do that'. It is always difficult to know which advice we should follow. Sometimes we are told two different things (as with the dress). Which should we believe? Our lives are full of these opposites and it is often difficult to know which is the truth. Even our closest friends can let us down and sometimes it is difficult to know who to believe. But God's advice is worth following and will not let us down.

These two readings were written hundreds of years apart, but in both cases the writers knew that when God spoke he was to be trusted! God speaks to Jeremiah and gives him the power to do the job. In the second reading, when Jesus speaks, a man is healed and his sins forgiven. Jeremiah 1.4–10:

The Lord said to me, 'I chose you before I gave you life, and before you were born I selected you to be a prophet to the nations.'

I answered, 'Sovereign Lord, I don't know how to speak; I am too young.'

But the Lord said to me, 'Do not say that you are too young, but go to the people I send you to, and tell them everything I command you to say. Do not be afraid of them, for I will be with you to protect you. I, the Lord, have spoken!'

Then the Lord stretched out his hand, touched my lips, and said to me, 'Listen, I am giving you the words you must speak. Today I give you authority over nations and kingdoms to uproot and to pull down, to destroy and to overthrow, to build and to plant.'

Matthew 9.1–7:

Jesus got into the boat and went back across the lake to his own town, where some people brought to him a paralysed man, lying on a bed. When Jesus saw how much faith they had, he said to the paralysed man, 'Courage, my son! Your sins are forgiven.'

Then some teachers of the Law said to themselves, 'This man is speaking blasphemy!'

Jesus perceived what they were thinking, so he said, 'Why are you thinking such evil things? Is it easier to say, "Your sins are forgiven," or to say, "Get up and walk"? I will prove to you, then, that the Son of Man has authority on earth to forgive sins.'

So he said to the paralysed man, 'Get up, pick up your bed, and go home!'

The man got up and went home.

Sing 'Be Still and Know' (*Mission Praise* 16) as a prayer.

RE
Following the ideas in the assembly explore ways that God speaks to people (through worship, conscience etc.). Ask questions like 'How do we know what we should or should not do?'

English
Look at 'authority', this time through verbal commands and language (e.g., by parents, grandparents, friends, teachers).

PE
Look at the rules of a competitive game and at the role of the referee. When and why are hand actions used instead of language?

Music
Explore the role of the conductor in music. Recognize different arm and hand instructions used by the conductor and find out their meaning.

God who loves (school or class assembly)

Another pattern found in the Old and New Testaments is the idea that God loves his people. This assembly looks at the evidence for God's love.

SCHOOL ASSEMBLY
In front of the pupils make some leaf prints on a large sheet of coloured paper, using one or more colours of paint. Alternatively, produce some pictures of prints made earlier. Use a variety of different leaves, and encourage pupils to try and identify the names of the different leaves.

CLASS ASSEMBLY
Allow pupils to make their own leaf prints. Alternatively, demonstrate how to make some.

Leaves, as we have seen, all make different patterns. If we have a knowledge of trees and know something about their leaves then we can identify the trees from the leaves, without needing to see the whole tree. (Some of us managed that!)

Similarly, people can be identified by their fingerprints, their footprints, and even their blood. We can also identify people in other ways. We say things like 'What a nice person they must be!', or 'Only a madman would do that!' We may not know someone, but the way they act leads us to guess something about the kind of person they might be.

If God could leave a print like a leaf print or a fingerprint, I wonder what that print would be? Can we think of anything in our world that would make us say 'I recognize God in that'?

In our theme this week we have been looking at patterns in the Bible. Another pattern can be seen in the way that men and women in the Bible recognized that God was present. They recognized that God loved his people and cared for them like a parent. God was sad when they did not listen. They recognized God's prints in this way everywhere.

Wherever there is evidence of love, God is present. 'Love' is the print that God leaves in the world.

From the Old Testament we hear what one person said about the love of God. Years later the writer of one of the New Testament books was to say something very similar: Psalm 103.1–4, 8:

Praise the Lord, my soul!
    All my being, praise his holy name!
Praise the Lord, my soul,
    and do not forget how kind he is.
He forgives all my sins
    and heals all my diseases.
He keeps me from the grave
    and blesses me with love and mercy . . .
The Lord is merciful and loving,
    slow to become angry and full of constant love.

1 John 4.7–10:

Dear friends, let us love one another, because love comes from God. Whoever loves is a child of God and knows God. Whoever does not love does not know God, for God is love. And God showed his love for us by sending his only Son into the world, so that we might have life through him. This is what love is: it is not that we have loved God, but that he loved us and sent his Son to be the means by which our sins are forgiven.

 (For school assembly.)
'When God made the garden of creation' (*BBC Complete Come and Praise* 16)

Conduct a Valentine meditation. It is called a Valentine Meditation because it is about love. Ask the pupils to close their eyes, before going through a short relaxation exercise.

If the pupils are new to this, conduct a short rehearsal. Ask them to close their eyes and to imagine a bird . . . and now to imagine that same bird walking through a doorway, or on top of a bus.

Once they have got the idea conduct the meditation, keeping the pace slow so that there is time for everyone to allow their imagination to work.

Think of a toy that you love or loved when you were younger.   What does it look like?   Can you feel it?   Try picking it up.   Can you play with the toy?   Or cuddle it?   Finally, if you wish, thank God for the toy that you loved.

Now think of an animal that you love, or that you once loved.   Is it a cat?   Or a dog?   Or a gerbil?   What is it?   Can you see what it looks like?   Can you touch it?   Where does it live?   What is its name?   Finally, if you wish, thank God for the animal.

Now think of someone you love.   Is it your Mother?   Or Father? Or a grandparent?   Perhaps it is a baby brother or sister.   Can you see them?   What do they feel like?   Do they cuddle you?   Or do you cuddle them?   Finally, if you wish, thank God for this person and for their love for you.

Close with these words:

Lord God,
We thank you for all the love in our lives,
    and for the evidence of your love for us.   Amen.

Allow the pupils a moment to come back to the present.

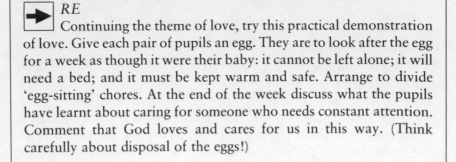

RE
Continuing the theme of love, try this practical demonstration of love. Give each pair of pupils an egg. They are to look after the egg for a week as though it were their baby: it cannot be left alone; it will need a bed; and it must be kept warm and safe. Arrange to divide 'egg-sitting' chores. At the end of the week discuss what the pupils have learnt about caring for someone who needs constant attention. Comment that God loves and cares for us in this way. (Think carefully about disposal of the eggs!)

English
Write letters to a friend about caring for the egg.

Design and technology
Design and make a bed or shelter for the egg.

PE
In groups of three or four, explore the mood and feeling of love in dance or movement.

God who calls us (class assembly)

Just as God loves his people, so he calls them to work in the world. It is our responsibility to identify and answer that call.

Ensure that all pupils *and* staff are seated. Inform them that when they hear themselves being called they are to stand up. Call out the following, emphasizing 'I now call . . .' each time. Eventually everyone will be standing!

Those called Mary or James.
Those with older brothers.
Those with glasses.

Those aged 6 and 9 years with birthdays this month.
Those with no fillings in their teeth.

Those called Louise or Robert.   Those with younger sisters.
Those who can drive.   Those who are male.
Those who are female.

Ask everyone to sit down.

In our lives we are called many times by many people. Sometimes we are called by our names, and sometimes in other ways. Often we answer the call, although sometimes we don't want to hear it and ignore the call. Always there is a choice for us.

Another pattern we find in the Bible involves the way God calls people to work for him. In the Old Testament, God called his prophets to go and speak to the people, and in the New Testament Jesus called the disciples to follow him. Each one answered the call. For the disciples it cannot have been an easy life, never knowing where the next meal would come from or whether the Romans or even the Pharisees would be hostile to them. They even had to leave their homes and their families to work for God. But when Jesus called they answered his call and followed him.

God still calls men, women, and children today. However, first we have to hear his call, and then we have to want to answer it—rather like the way I called you a few moments ago! Sometimes he uses our conscience to call us; sometimes he speaks through other people. There are many ways that God speaks to us, and we must constantly listen out for his call.

Here are two stories about people being called by God. First, in the Old Testament we hear how God calls Abram to be the Father of a nation, and despite his age Abram obeys! Then in the New Testament we hear about Jesus calling a rich young man to follow him. Here, however, things are different. Genesis 12.1–4:

The Lord said to Abram, 'Leave your country, your relatives and your father's home, and go to a land that I am going to show you. I will give you many descendants, and they will become a great nation. I will bless you and make your name famous, so that you will be a blessing.

I will bless those who bless you,

But I will curse those who curse you.

And through you I will bless all the nations.'

When Abram was seventy-five years old, he started out from Haran, as the Lord had told him to do; and Lot went with him.

Matthew 19.16–24:

Once a man came to Jesus. 'Teacher,' he asked, 'What good thing must I do to receive eternal life?'

'Why do you ask me concerning what is good?' answered Jesus. 'There is only One who is good. Keep the commandments if you want to enter life.'

'What commandments?' he asked.

Jesus answered, 'Do not commit murder; do not commit adultery; do not steal; do not accuse anyone falsely; respect your father and your mother; and love your neighbour as you love yourself.'

'I have obeyed all these commandments,' the young man replied. 'What else do I need to do?'

Jesus said to him, 'If you want to be perfect, go and sell all you have and give the money to the poor, and you will have riches in heaven; then come and follow me.'

When the young man heard this, he went away sad, because he was very rich.

Jesus then said to his disciples, 'I assure you: it will be very hard for rich people to enter the Kingdom of heaven. I repeat: it is much harder for a rich person to enter the Kingdom of God than for a camel to go through the eye of a needle.'

Lord God,
We thank you that you call people to follow you,
    and that they're ready, like Abram,
    to do your work.
We pray for those like the rich young man
    who cannot follow you.
We pray for ourselves that we may continue
    to hear your call to follow you.   Amen.

RE
Continue looking at the way God calls people by exploring vocation. What different kinds of work are people called to do?

History
Study monasteries and churches as an extension study, with particular attention to monks and clergy and their calling. This would be particularly suitable if the class are studying the study unit on Life in Tudor Times.

English
Create poetry on 'The Call'.

God to the rescue (school or class assembly)

Often we find ourselves out of our depth and in need of help. A pattern that often occurs in the Bible is that of God coming to rescue his people. This assembly looks at how we might get help when we need it.

Note: Do not mention this theme before completing the activity.

 Set up one or two role-play sketches. For example:

SKETCH I

Two people rowing a boat that is beginning to sink. One of the two keeps rowing while the other starts bailing out water. Things begin to get desperate, so both start bailing.

(Ask the question: How can they get help?
Answers might be: Use a flare, or signal SOS with a torch or radio. Someone seeing them on shore could dial 999 and ask for the Coast Guard.)

SKETCH 2

Two people asleep. They wake to find the room filled with smoke. They hold handkerchiefs over their mouths and crawl along the floor towards the door. On opening the door they find there are flames on the other side.

(Ask the question: How should they get help?
Answers might be: Dial 999 and ask for the Fire Brigade.)

Sometimes in our lives we need urgent help and we should all know how to get that help. We usually dial 999 and ask for the Police, Fire Brigade, Ambulance, or Coast Guard. At sea we might also set off a distress flare or broadcast SOS. Any of these actions will bring help, and the lives of many people are saved each year.

But there is one other thing we can do. We can call on God for help. For thousands of years men and women have shouted to God for help in times of trouble. We can call these shouts 'arrow' prayers. They are prayers sent to God in times of emergency, prayers like 'Please God, get me out of here!' or 'God! Help me!' Some of the psalms are like this.

God does not always answer our prayers in quite the way that we want, but he does always answer them. Don't forget that an answer can sometimes be 'No!' Either way, we must not forget to say 'Thank you!'

Today's readings both involve cries for help. The first is a psalm, one of the greatest cries for help that has ever been written. In the second, Jesus hears the cry of the lepers and heals them, but only one remembers to come back and thank him. Psalm 57.1–5:

Be merciful to me, O God, be merciful,
    because I come to you for safety.
In the shadow of your wings I find protection
    until the raging storms are over.

I call to God, the Most High,
    to God, who supplies my every need.
He will answer from heaven and save me;
    he will defeat my oppressors.
God will show me his constant love and faithfulness.

I am surrounded by enemies,
    who are like man-eating lions.
Their teeth are like spears and arrows;
    their tongues are like sharp swords.

Show your greatness in the sky, O God,
    and your glory over all the earth.

Luke 17.11–19:

As Jesus made his way to Jerusalem, he went along the border between Samaria and Galilee. He was going into a village when he was met by ten men suffering from a dreaded skin-disease. They stood at a distance, and shouted, 'Jesus! Master! Take pity on us!'

Jesus saw them and said to them, 'Go and let the priests examine you.'

On the way they were made clean. When one of them saw that he was healed, he came back, praising God in a loud voice. He threw himself to the ground at Jesus' feet and thanked him. The man was a Samaritan. Jesus said, 'There were ten men who were healed; where are the other nine? Why is this foreigner the only one who came back to give thanks to God?' And Jesus said to him, 'Get up and go; your faith has made you well.'

 (For school assembly.)
'The Lord's my shepherd' (*BBC Complete Come and Praise* 56)

Lord God,
So often we try to get ourselves out of trouble
    only to find that we get further into trouble.
  Help us to remember that you wait for us to turn to you,
    and that your loving arms are always there to help us.   Amen.

RE
Follow up the assembly by looking at Psalm 61.1 or 69.1–3. Talk about times when pupils have felt in danger. Who did they turn to for protection?

Art
Still looking at protection, use the imagery of Psalm 57.1 as a stimulus for creating artwork.

History
If suitable, as part of the study unit on Life in Tudor Times look at the custom of sanctuary (see Deuteronomy 4.41–43). Find out about Thomas à Becket's murder.

Design and Technology
Design a place of sanctuary or retreat in the school or classroom. Who might use it, and when? What facilities would be needed?

INVESTIGATIONS

The theme of this week's assemblies will allow pupils to investigate the Church and the Bible in greater depth. The content of the assemblies will provide opportunities for follow-up work across the curriculum.

The Church: 1 (school assembly)

The Church has meant a great deal to many people over the centuries. This assembly is designed to stimulate investigation further, and to encourage a sense of thankfulness.

Hold a 'word hunt'. Ask pupils to find as many words that *sound the same*, but have different *meanings* (i.e., they often have different spellings). For example:

Bear: an animal
Bare: no clothes/nothing on

Cross: two pieces of material placed one across the other
Cross: irritated

Gather as many words as possible, and list them on an over-head projector or board. Alternatively, you could offer a selection of mixed words to include many that sound the same but have different meanings. Ask pupils to pick out those that match and try to explain the different meanings. Possible examples: to/too/two; dear/deer; cross/cross; their/there; see/sea.

All the words we have been looking at have at least two different meanings. They sound the same, but they do not mean the same thing. Another such word with two meanings is the word *church*. It means a building (give an example of a local church building), *and* it means people who meet together for worship. So a church could mean people who meet together in a house, *or* those who meet in . . . (mention a local well-known church).

Optional: Invite a visitor in to speak about activities in a local church.

In the New Testament we read about the new church—a large group of people meeting wherever they can find to meet. Acts 2.43–47:

> Many miracles and wonders were being done through the apostles, and everyone was filled with awe. All the believers continued together in close fellowship and shared their belongings with one another. They would sell their property and possessions, and distribute the money among all, according to what each one needed. Day after day they met as a group in the Temple, and they had their meals together in their homes, eating with glad and humble hearts, praising God, and

enjoying the good will of all the people. And every day the Lord added to their group those who were being saved.

 'At the name of Jesus' (*BBC Complete Come and Praise* 58)

 Lord God,
    We thank you for the gift of your Church,
        and for all Christians throughout the world.
    We pray especially for those who have just been baptized,
        and for those who have lost their faith.
    We pray also for the members of —— (local church/es)
        and for those who are Christians in this school.   Amen.

 To follow up the assembly, visit a local church and carry out any of the following.

RE
Sit in silence in the church and ask pupils to use their senses: what can they smell, see, hear, feel?

History
Investigate tombs, memorial tablets and gravestones at the church. What information can be found out about the past?

Art
Sketch different architectural aspects of the church visited (e.g., arches, windows, roofs, pillars).

Mathematics
Identify common shapes found in the church—cubes, rectangles, hexagons, circles etc. Explore patterns found on floors or in windows. Make 2-D or 3-D shapes of those found.

Music
Listen to some early church music (e.g., Gregorian chant), and then some modern church music (e.g., music by Graham Kendrick). Talk about differences or similarities.

The Church 2: (class assembly)

This assembly continues the theme of investigating the Church and looks at those people who work for the Church.

Ask the class how many people (or jobs) they can identify who might work for the local church. This activity could be carried out by the whole class, or done in pairs. The final list might include:

minister	cleaner	builder
organist	curate	prayer leaders
deacon	choristers	flower-arranger
bookseller	embroiderers	bell-ringers
churchwardens	sick visitors	Sunday school leaders
server	grave-digger	gardener
		healers

In the New Testament St Paul speaks about those people who work for the Church as being the 'different parts of the body of Christ'. 1 Corinthians 12.27–31a:

All of you are Christ's body, and each one is a part of it. In the church God has put all in place: in the first place apostles, in the second place prophets, and in the third place teachers; then those who perform miracles, followed by those who are given the power to heal or to help others or to direct them or to speak in strange tongues. They are not all apostles or prophets or teachers. Not everyone has the power to work miracles or to heal diseases or to speak in strange tongues or to explain what is said. Set your hearts, then, on the more important gifts.

Lord God,
We thank you for those who work for your Church:
    for all who lead worship,
    teach the young,
    visit the sick,
    or look after your Church in so many different ways.
We pray especially for all clergy, particularly —— (local clergy)
    and give thanks for their work and life.   Amen.

This assembly could be explored further in a variety of ways across the curriculum. See follow-up ideas for the previous assembly 'Church: 1'.

Worship (school assembly)

This assembly allows for some further exploration of what it means to worship God in church and in school.

Today we are investigating the subject of the Church and worship. We are going to look at what we do when we worship God. Our assemblies are acts of worship, so are services held in church—but what are they all about?

There are many things in our lives, and many people, that we may think of as being special and important (our parents or brothers and sisters, our bike or other toys, etc.) but we do not usually think of them as being the most important things in the whole world. Only God should be that special, for God made all the world and looks after us throughout our life. So in worship we speak to God our Maker, we praise and thank God, we learn more about God, and we ask God's help for other people. In our worship today we shall look further at these.

With the help of two pupils (more could be used) and a member of staff, continue the assembly as follows.

It might help if the words 'praise', 'confession', 'learning', and 'intercession' were put up on a board or over-head projector as they occur.

Pupil 1: Worship is about *praise*. Praise means saying how wonderful someone is. We praise people when they do something special, like saving someone from drowning, or when they do very well in an exam. We praise God when we speak about the wonderful things God has done for us.

Pupil 2: We shall now sing —— which is a hymn of praise. Listen to what it says about God. (Use a hymn of praise like 'Jubilate Deo' from *Mission Praise*, or another suitable song of praise.)

Pupil 1: Worship is about *confession*. Confession means saying we are sorry for all the things we have done wrong.

Pupil 2: Let's spend a moment in silence thinking of all the things we have done which we are now sorry about.

(*Silence*)

> Lord God,
> Forgive us for our sins.
> We are sorry that we have hurt you.
> Help us to start again, and try to be the person you want us to be.
> Amen.

Pupil 1: Worship is about *learning*. We listen to stories from the Bible and we learn about God and the way that God wants us to live.

Member of staff: This reading is taken from the Old Testament. The Jews have been chosen as God's people and have been given rules by which to live. Moses reminds the people of the most important rule of all. Deuteronomy 6.1–9:

'These are all the laws that the Lord your God commanded me to teach you. Obey them in the land that you are about to enter and occupy. As long as you live, you and your descendants are to honour the Lord your God and obey all his laws that I am giving you, so that you may live in that land a long time. Listen to them, people of Israel, and obey them! Then all will go well with you, and you will become a mighty nation and live in that rich and fertile land, just as the Lord, the God of our ancestors, has promised.

'Israel, remember this! The Lord—and the Lord alone—is our God. Love the Lord your God with all your heart, with all your soul, and with all your strength. Never forget these commands that I am giving you today. Teach them to your children. Repeat them when you are at home and when you are away, when you are resting and when you are working. Tie them on your arms and wear them on your foreheads as a reminder. Write them on the door-posts of your houses and on your gates.

Pupil 1: Worship is also about *intercession*. Intercession means asking God to help someone.

(Use slides or large pictures of any of the following for the intercessions: a church building; people in need in another part of the world; someone ill in hospital or the picture of a nurse. Put up the pictures as each prayer is read, so that pupils may choose to keep their eyes open.)

Pupil 2: Today we pray for your Church, and we remember especially those people who are being persecuted for their faith. We also pray for local churches, their clergy and people. Lord, in your mercy,

   All: Hear our prayer.

Pupil 1: We pray for people across the world who have no food or homes, and we remember especially children who are in danger. Lord, in your mercy,

   All: Hear our prayer.

Pupil 2: We pray for those in hospital, and those who are ill. We remember especially children from this school who are ill. Lord, in your mercy,

All: Hear our prayer.

Pupil 1: We close our act of worship today by saying the words of the Grace. (If necessary say 'Please repeat after me'.)

The grace of our Lord Jesus Christ,
and the love of God
and the fellowship of the Holy Spirit
be with us all evermore.   Amen.

 RE
Continue the work on worship started in the assembly by learning another famous prayer, for example, the Lord's Prayer (see *The Lord's Prayer for Children Retold*). Alternatively, find out about the Communion service (e.g., what happens, who initiated it and why).

English
Discuss further the meaning of the word 'worship' (e.g., the giving of worth). What does the 'developed' world seem to hold 'in worthship' (money, cars etc.)? Compare this to other parts of the world, and use as the basis for some creative work.

Music
Continue to think about worship by listening to some music for the Anglican service of Evensong or for a Eucharist (e.g., one of Stanford's settings of the Magnificat or part of a Haydn Mass). Discuss the use of the music and the setting for which it was written. Alternatively, listen to a tape of some modern music for worship (e.g., Taizé chant or a musical by Roger Jones).

Art
Look at pictures of triptychs and find out about artwork used in worship. Visit a local church to look at a triptych in position.

The Bible: 1 (school assembly)

This assembly looks at the Bible, and investigates its use as an instruction book for Christians to use in their daily living, as well as its use in church.

Take some packets of different seeds, a number of pots or trays, and sufficient compost and water to plant the seeds. Ensure there are a number of different types of seed (bean seeds, sunflower seeds, mustard and cress etc.), all needing different conditions in which to grow. Show pupils the different seeds and explain which is which seed.

Ask some pupils to come and help plant the seeds. One pupil should read out the necessary planting instructions from the back of the packet (these could be written out on separate cards).

As the seeds are planted encourage pupils to see that the plants have different instructions, that they will grow at different rates, and will eventually produce totally different results. Point out that without the instructions you might have planted them all at the same depth and put them all in the sun—whereas some might need semi-shade or protection in a greenhouse!

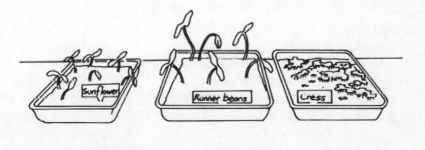

In the same way that we need to read the instructions to find out how best to grow seeds, so we need to read instructions to find out how we should grow as human beings—not how we should grow taller, but how we should grow into the kind of person that God wants us to become.

The best instruction book is the Bible. (You may wish to hold up a Bible.) In here there is all the information we need. This Bible has a lot to teach us, if we are ready to follow its instructions, which is why the

Church uses the Bible to help Christians to learn more about God and about how God wants them to live.

Listen to what the writer of this psalm says about the Bible. Psalm 119.97–99, 105–106:

How I love your law!
　I think about it all day long.
Your commandment is with me all the time
　and makes me wiser than my enemies.
I understand more than all my teachers,
　because I meditate on your instructions . . .
Your word is a lamp to guide me
　and a light for my path.
I will keep my solemn promise
　to obey your just instructions.

'Our Father, who art in heaven' (*BBC Complete Come and Praise* 51)

Hold up a large copy of the Bible:

Lord God,
We thank you for the gift of your word,
　and for all those who were inspired to write your book.
Help us to learn more about you
　so that we may continue growing like
　healthy seeds in good soil.　　Amen.

RE
Follow up the assembly by exploring the contents of the Bible, for example, as a library of books.

Art
Write out verses or initial letters of the Lord's Prayer rather in the style of a medieval manuscript, with the initial letter decorated.

History
Explore the development of the Bible: the languages first used, the discovery of the Dead Sea Scrolls, first English copy etc.

Music
Listen to the story of Mary Jones and her Bible in *Greater than Gold* by Roger Jones.

Geography
Continuing the idea of following instructions, use an Ordnance Survey walker's map (1:25000) to create a circular walk in the neighbourhood suitable for a family. Try out the walk.

IT
Put the instructions for the walk onto a word processor and print.

The Bible: 2 (class assembly)

This assembly continues the theme of the previous one, and looks at the Bible as a treasure house to be explored.

Collect as many different Bibles as possible, to include different editions and illustrated Bibles, as well as Bibles in a variety of sizes. You may need to remind the pupils that some books are valuable or delicate.

Encourage the pupils to work in small groups and to find out as much as possible about the Bibles they are handling. Ask questions like:

- When was your Bible printed?
- What language is it printed in?
- Describe the Bible (as though to a blind person).
- How many books are there in the Bible (the presence or absence of the Apocrypha will make a difference to the answer)?
- Find out the name of any of the following in your Bible:

— a book of history
— a book of poetry
— a book of songs
— a book of letters
— a book about someone's life.

The Bible is a whole library of books, as we have seen. It contains history books about the Jewish people, a book of songs to be sung in church or synagogue, some books of letters about a new church, and other books about the life of Jesus the Son of God. Above all, it is a book about God and his people. It is also a book to be 'treasured' and looked after, and a book to be kept safe and read.

(Open one of the Bibles and place in a prominent position in the classroom for pupils to look at during the rest of the day.)

The reading today is very famous, and shows Jesus teaching his listeners how to pray. Matthew 6.9–13:

'This, then, is how you should pray:

"Our Father in heaven:
    may your holy name be honoured;
    may your Kingdom come;
    may your will be done on earth as it is in heaven.
Give us today the food we need.
Forgive us the wrongs we have done,
    as we forgive the wrongs that others have done to us.
Do not bring us to hard testing,
    but keep us safe from the Evil One."'

Encourage each group to be silent for a moment, and then ask different pupils to read the different sentences of the prayer if appropriate:

Lord God,
We pray for all those who cannot see to read,
  and for those who are unable to read.   (*pause*)

We pray for all who wish to learn more about you,
  but who live in countries where Bibles are expensive,
  or where they cannot read the Bible
  in their own language.   (*pause*)

We pray for the work of SPCK
  and other organizations who provide Bibles
  for people throughout the world.   (*pause*)   Amen.

This assembly could be explored further in a variety of ways within the classroom. See follow-up ideas in the previous assembly, 'The Bible: 1'.

Week 9

CHANGE

The philosopher Immanuel Kant once said, 'To grow is to change'. We are all subject to change in our lives from the moment of our birth, but the way that we meet change will be different for each of us. The assembly theme this week endeavours to look at ways of responding to changes in our lives.

We can change (school assembly)

This assembly looks at the way that things change. We are reminded that humans change and, with God's help, can change for the better.

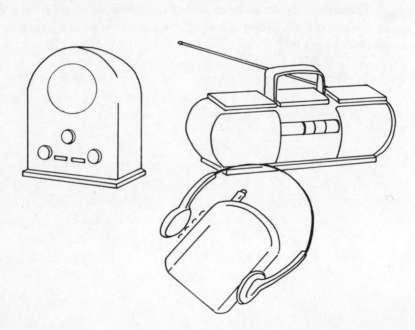

Invite three people to help with this assembly. Each person is to speak about a radio, and where possible to bring an example of the radio with them. Comment that you are going to look at the changes that have occurred to radios this century, and have asked some people to help you. The following is an example of how this session might go:

> *Mr X (approx. 65 years)*: 'When I was young I listened to music on a *crystal set* which I made myself . . . (continues to explain what a crystal set was, how it was made, difficulties of reception, etc.).

> *Mrs Y (approx. 50 years)*: 'When I was young I listened to rock and roll on Radio Luxembourg/Radio Caroline on my *wireless* . . . (continues to explain what the wireless looked like, its size etc., or produces one to show pupils as she talks).

> *Child (pupil from school)*: 'I am young, and I listen to Radio —— (local radio) on my Walkman . . . (shows all those present the Walkman, and explains about its portability, reception, cost etc.).

———————————

In just a few years great changes have taken place all around us. Cars have changed shape, electronic games have come and then gone out of fashion, and even people have changed. As we have seen, the radio started as a fairly simple piece of equipment that could be made by most boys and girls on their own. But since then it has changed into something so sophisticated that it has to be made by experts.

In the same way, changes occur to people over a period of time. We can change our appearance—grow taller, alter the colour of our hair, or become slimmer or smaller. In particular, as we grow from a child into an adult, many changes take place to our bodies.

Changes also occur in other ways. For instance, God created humans to be loving and kind, but all too often we are anything but kind. At some time or other, all of us have been selfish and unkind. However we *can* change into what God intended. Just as a radio can be improved so we too, with God's help, can change for the better.

Today's story is about someone who changed and was forgiven— even at the last moment of his life: Luke 23.32–34, 39–43:

> Two other men, both of them criminals, were also led out to be put to death with Jesus. When they came to the place called 'The Skull', they crucified Jesus there, and the two criminals, one on his right and one on his left. Jesus said, 'Forgive them, Father! They don't know what they are doing.' . . .

115

One of the criminals hanging there hurled insults at him: 'Aren't you the Messiah? Save yourself and us!'

The other one, however, rebuked him, saying 'Don't you fear God? You received the same sentence he did. Ours, however, is only right because we are getting what we deserve for what we did; but he has done no wrong.' And he said to Jesus, 'Remember me, Jesus, when you come as King!'

Jesus said to him, 'I promise you that today you will be in Paradise with me.'

 'One more step along the world I go' (*BBC Complete Come and Praise* 47)

 Encourage 'eyes open' prayer, and use a lump of play dough on a board to focus attention. During the prayer carry out the actions as shown:

Lord God,
You made us perfect   (*start with a round ball of dough*),
  but we have ruined your work   (*tear the dough apart*).
We try to live our life in our own   (*continue tearing*),
  way and so often we are wrong.
We try to love you and each   (*two pieces join up*),
  other but all too often we
  end up hating everyone   (*two pieces torn apart*).
Teach us how to change ourselves   (*begin to put all the dough together*),
  so that we may once more
  stand before you as complete   (*smooth round ball*).
Amen.

→ *History*
If the class are working on the study unit Britain since 1930, follow up the assembly by looking at changes during the lives of the pupils (clothes, the family, toys etc.). Mount a collection of photographs on 'How we have changed'.

Science
Experiment with mixing, heating, or cooling materials to discover which change, and which changes can or cannot be reversed.

RE
Tell the story of *The Cross and the Switchblade* by David Wilkerson. Make New Year or Lenten resolutions (e.g., 'I will no longer . . . , but I will . . .').

Mathematics
Continue with the subject of change in Mathematics by looking at place values or division by powers of 10. Ask what changes occur.

Continual change (class assembly)

This assembly explores the need for all humans to change. We cannot remain still on our journey of life, no matter how much we might like to stay the same.

Mrs. Woodward   Mr. Zahiv   Mr. Hughes

In the week before the assembly, obtain some photographs of people known to the pupils (staff, dinner ladies, lollipop person, parents, or even some of the pupils), when they were babies.

117

Give all the photographs a number on the back and keep the 'key' to hand. Then divide the class into groups, and give each group one or two photographs. Allow them a few moments to guess the identity of the babies.

The groups could then pass their pictures onto a new group, to continue the game. Finally, give the answer to each group.

Throughout our lives we continually grow. Each day and each night as we sleep we are growing. We might be growing bigger—physically—or even, as we get older, smaller. Our hair and our nails keep on growing even when we are asleep. We never stop growing in one way or another, until the day that we die (and a little thereafter, though you might not want to mention this!).

To grow is to change! We never stay the same. It is not just our body that keeps changing as it grows; our mind changes each day as we learn new things. Change is in fact the most natural thing in the world.

However, sometimes we would like to stay the same. Perhaps we do not like new things that happen to us, like going to a new school or losing a friend. God understands this, but all the same he expects us to move on in our journey of life. We cannot stand still; there are new things to look forward to just round the corner.

Jesus knew all about people who did not want to change. The Pharisees, in particular, did not want things to change. For instance, they were concerned that Jesus was breaking the law even when he was healing people. Here is what happened during one of these clashes. Luke 6.6–11:

On another Sabbath Jesus went into a synagogue and taught. A man was there whose right hand was paralysed. Some teachers of the Law and some Pharisees wanted a reason to accuse Jesus of doing wrong, so they watched him closely to see if he would heal on the Sabbath. But Jesus knew their thoughts and said to the man, 'Stand up and come here to the front.' The man got up and stood there. Then Jesus said to them, 'I ask you: What does our Law allow us to do on the Sabbath? To help or to harm? To save a man's life or destroy it?' He looked round at them all; then he said to the man, 'Stretch out your hand.' He did so, and his hand became well again.

They were filled with rage and began to discuss among themselves what they could do to Jesus.

Leader: Lord God,
        Each day we change and grow,
All: and you care for us continually.
Leader: Each day we learn new facts,
All: and you care for us continually.
Leader: Each day we gain new experience,
All: and you care for us continually.
Leader: Continue to guard us as we grow towards maturity.
All: Amen.

RE
Follow up the story by finding out more about the Pharisees. Read about their opposition to Jesus (e.g., Luke 6.1–5 or 18.9–14). Alternatively, explore changes in life (e.g., the death of an animal, moving house, being ill), and talk about the joys and woes of change.

Science
The assembly reminded us that our bodies change: look at nutrition, and the food needed for energy and growth.

English
Read the story of Peter Pan and talk about 'the boy who didn't want to grow up'. Or, read the story *The Surprise Present* by Elaine Brown.

Our environment (school assembly)

The world can be a beautiful place, but humans can change that. This assembly reminds us of our responsibilities to our environment, and reminds us what God's world once looked like.

ROLE-PLAY

Arrange for a group of pupils to enter the room when everyone else is in place. They should surreptitiously drop items of 'clean' rubbish (crisp packets, clean tissues, paper etc.), while appearing not to notice their actions.

Continue by role-playing the following between two teachers, or a teacher and a child, along the lines of the following:

First person: Why is there rubbish on the floor?
Second person: Is there? I hadn't noticed.
First person: Well look at this. (*picks up piece of rubbish*)
Second person: Oh! So there is!
First person: Where did it come from?
Second person: . . . etc.

Allow the role-play to continue as desired, perhaps looking at the whole school and its environment.

THE CONTRACT

Talk to the pupils about how they feel the school *should* look, and how it might have looked when it was first built. Ask who is actually responsible for which parts of the school, and for what work:

We the pupils of St. Martin's School
are responsible for picking up paper rubbish
inside and outside the school,
We are also responsible for looking after the
wild garden,
and will maintain this to the best of our ability.
We also agree to

- For instance, is it the responsibility of the caretaker (or cleaners) to pick up sweet and tissue papers?
- Who is responsible for cleaning dirty marks off the walls?
- Who is responsible for cutting the grass or weeding the flower beds?
- Who is responsible for putting away books?

Finally, make a list of jobs/areas that pupils can take responsibility for, listing them on a board or over-head projector. Arrange for this to be produced for permanent display later.

In the book of Genesis we see how an early civilization thought that God might have made the world. Most Christians now believe that the creation of the world took millions of years, although God was involved in making this wonderful universe throughout this time. God is still working on his creation today.

Rather like our school—of which we are proud—the world can be a beautiful place. Unfortunately all too often we treat the world like a rubbish dump throwing away the things we do not want and making it dirty. We pollute our rivers and the sea, poison the air, and destroy the forests and countryside.

We are all responsible for keeping our environment as beautiful as possible.

Listen to this story, and try to imagine how beautiful the world must have been at first, before human beings began to change it. Genesis 1.20–24, 27–31:

Then God commanded, 'Let the water be filled with many kinds of living beings, and let the air be filled with birds.' So God created the great sea-monsters, all kinds of creatures that live in the water, and all kinds of birds. And God was pleased with what he saw. He blessed them all and told the creatures that live in the water to reproduce, and to fill the sea, and he told the birds to increase in number. Evening passed and morning came—that was the fifth day.

Then God commanded, 'Let the earth produce all kinds of animal life: domestic and wild, large and small.' . . . So God created human beings, making them to be like himself. He created them male and female, blessed them, and said, 'Have many children, so that your descendants will live all over the earth and bring it under their control. I am putting you in charge of the fish, the birds, and all the wild animals. I have provided all kinds of grain and all kinds of fruit for you to eat; but for all the wild animals and for all the birds I have provided grass and leafy plants for food'—and it was done. God looked at everything he had made, and he was very pleased.

Lord God,
We thank you for our beautiful world,
    for the colours of the sky and the sounds of the sea,
    for the smell of flowers and the taste of fruit,
    for trees and birds and animals.
Forgive us for ruining your world,
    and for turning it into a rubbish tip:
    for poisoning the rivers and the air,
    and for neglecting to look after your creation.
Help us to play our part in making this world a better place to
    live.   Amen.

'When God made the garden of creation' (*BBC Complete Come and Praise* 16)

Science
Follow up the ideas concerned with pollution in the assembly by conducting a survey on any waste or common land over a few square metres of ground to obtain evidence about pollution. Sort and categorize items found. (See also page 3 on pollution.)

RE
Begin a collection of waste material to raise money for charity (e.g., paper, tin foil or stamps). Find out about Greenpeace (see Useful Addresses).

Art
Explore how waste material can be used in art, by making a collage out of waste products.

English
Read *The Iron Woman* by Ted Hughes.

Changing families (class assembly)

This assembly looks at changes that occur to families, as the focus for thanksgiving prayer.

Explore the idea of the family tree with pupils. Put up the following names on an overhead projector or board, and ask the class to use these to create a family tree for the British Royal family:

	Philip	Elizabeth	
Charles	Anne	Andrew	Edward
Diana	Mark	Sarah	
	Timothy		
William	Peter	Beatrice	
Harry	Zara	Eugenie	

Families come in lots of different shapes and sizes as we have seen with the Royal Family, and any one family is a constantly changing group of people. It never stays the same for long. People get married, have children, or die, and in a few years a family can be different.

One of the greatest families mentioned in the Old Testament is Abram's. God promised Abram that he would become the father of a whole nation, with as many people in it as the stars in the sky. God also promised that Abram would have a country to settle in.

Sarah laughed at God's promise, for she knew she was too old to have children. But God knew what was possible and Sarah did have a child, and from him Abram's great family was born.

Today we think about Abram and his family at the beginning of their great adventure, and as we think of him we thank God for our own families.

This is the very beginning of the story of Abram and his family, starting with his father Terah. Genesis 11.27–32:

These are the descendants of Terah, who was the father of Abram, Nahor, and Haran. Haran was the father of lot, and Haran died in his native city, Ur in Babylonia, while his father was still living. Abram married Sarai, and Nahor married Milcah, the daughter of Haran, who was also the father of Iscah. Sarai was not able to have children.

Terah took his son Abram, his grandson Lot, who was the son of Haran, and his daughter-in-law Sarai, Abram's wife, and with them he left the city of Ur in Babylonia to go to the land of Canaan. They went as far as Haran and settled there. Terah died there at the age of two hundred and five.

 Use a picture of a family to act as a focus, and encourage all the pupils to look at their family trees (even if they are not completed) and to think about the people they represent. As each person is mentioned, they should think of those in their own family, thanking God for them in their hearts.

Lord God,
We thank you for our parents,
    for their *love* and care for us.   (*pause*)

We thank you for our brothers and sisters,
    for their *friendship* and care for us.   (*pause*)

We thank you for our grandparents,
    for their *support* and care for us.   (*pause*) Amen.

History
Follow up the idea of family trees by creating a family tree for the Royal Family starting with Edward VII.

RE
Create 'life-lines'. List the events in each pupil's life on a pathway, going up or down according to how good or bad the event felt to each pupil.

Art
Encourage pupils to finish researching their own family trees, then paint these onto 'parchment'. Affix a 'seal' so that they resemble an official document.

God is changeless (school or class assembly)

The last few assemblies have looked at change. This assembly is concerned with the changelessness of God.

Examine material that has been weathered (e.g., stones, wood, or glass worn by either air or water). Allow pupils to handle the items if possible.

Discuss how long the weathering process might have taken, and what aspect of the weather might have caused the deterioration. Produce examples of new material that has as yet sustained no weathering (e.g., a new brick or piece of wood). What other things might cause damage to these materials (e.g., fire, humans)?

All materials can be affected by the weather—by wind, rain, snow and frost—as well as by fire or earthquake. Comment on any local buildings that are badly affected by weathering, for example, a cathedral or church. Conclude that *nothing* that we can make with our hands is permanent, neither is anything in our world—mountains, trees, rivers. All can and do change.

The Bible reminds us that there is only one thing in the world that is permanent and unchanging—God. God is like someone who loves us no matter what we have done, and we can never destroy that love; it too is permanent and unchanging.

The psalmist reminds us that no matter what happens in our world, God is always with us. This story reminds us that no matter what the son in the story has done, the father is still there ready to welcome him back. Luke 15.11–24:

Jesus went on to say, 'There was once a man who had two sons. The younger one said to him, "Father, give me my share of the property now." So the man divided his property between his two sons. After a few days the younger son sold his part of the property and left home with the money. He went to a country far away, where he wasted his money in reckless living. He spent everything he had. Then a severe famine spread over that country, and he was left without a thing. So he went to work for one of the citizens of that country, who sent him out to his farm to take care of the pigs. He wished he could fill himself with the bean pods the pigs ate, but no one gave him anything to eat. At last he came to his senses and said, "All my father's hired workers have more than they can eat, and here am I about to starve! I will get up and go to my father and say, Father, I have sinned against God and against you. I am no longer fit to be called your son; treat me as one of your hired workers." So he got up and started back to his father.

'He was still a long way from home when his father saw him; his heart was filled with pity, and he ran, threw his arms round his son, and kissed him. "Father," the son said, "I have sinned against God and against you. I am no longer fit to be called your son." But the father called his servants. "Hurry!" he said. "Bring the best robe and put it on him. Put a ring on his finger and shoes on his feet. Then go and get the prize calf and kill it, and let us celebrate with a feast! For this son of mine was dead, but now he is alive; he was lost, but now he has been found." And so the feasting began.'

(For school assembly.)
'Guess how I feel' (*BBC Complete Come and Praise* 89)

Lord God,
We know that nothing in our world is permanent,
and that the strongest buildings
do not last for ever.

Everything we make is subject to decay,
  even the world in which we live.
Help us to remember
  that although everything around us changes you are unchanging,
  and always with us.   Amen.

RE

Pursuing the idea of God as unchanging, give out verses of Psalm 139 to pupils. Allow them to live with their verse for a day or two. What does the verse mean to them? Encourage pupils to choose a picture to go with their verse. Then find a piece of music to accompany the psalm and listen to it with pupils holding up their pictures at the correct time.

Art

Create 'illuminated manuscripts' based on the verses of Psalm 139 allocated to each pupil.

History

As part of the study unit on Romans, Anglo-Saxons and Vikings, or the study unit on Life in Tudor Times, find out about monks and illustrated manuscripts.

Geography

Follow up the look at weathering by making a study of the locality and look at the effects of weather on school and church buildings.

Week 10

EVIDENCE

How do we know if we are living the kind of life God wants us to live? What evidence can we show that we are doing what God wants? The next five assemblies suggest what evidence to look for in our lives.

Love (school or class assembly)

Jesus taught his disciples to live a very different life to that which most people lived. This assembly looks at one of the major pieces of evidence to be found if we are really following in Jesus' footsteps.

I expect we have all met people who say one thing but do another. For instance, they say that they are your best friend, but then they are really horrible to you! They come round to your home, but then say nasty things about you behind your back the next day.

Jesus taught people that they should lead a very different kind of life to this. He taught them that they should be kind and loving to each other, and that they should treat others as they would like to be treated themselves.

But the question is—how do we know if we are actually living this kind of life? What evidence do we have that tells us we are doing things correctly? (You may need to explain the meaning of the word evidence.)

One piece of evidence is that we *love* one another. Jesus said we must love one another in the same way that we love ourselves. (You might want to comment that this kind of love is not the same as 'falling in love'; it is like the love that a parent shows for their child.) We do not go around hurting ourselves, so we should not hurt each other. We do not shout at ourselves, so we should not shout at others. Everything we like done to us, we should do to others. If we like people to be friends with us, then we must be friends with others.

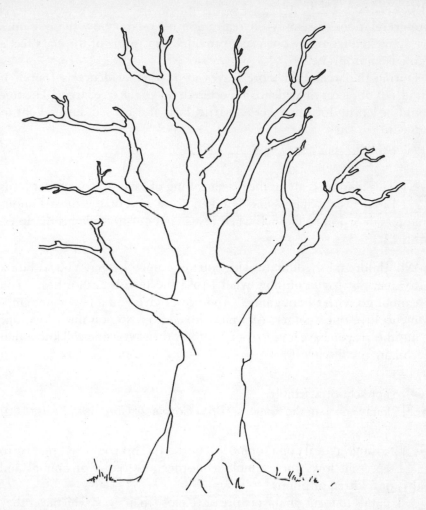

Before the assembly, put up a picture of a large tree with trunk and branches, but with no leaves. It could be made from sugar-paper or card, and should be big enough for everyone to see easily. You will also need a large quantity of paper leaves and some glue.

Explain that the tree is going to help show all of us if we are really trying to live the kind of life that God wants his people to live. Every time anyone in the school shows any evidence that they are loving others as they do themselves then a leaf will be added to the tree.

Encourage teachers *and* pupils to mention anyone who has already shown this evidence, and stick a leaf on the tree. Note, leaves should be added for pupils and teachers. This should not become a kind of 'congratulations' assembly—it really doesn't matter how many names are suggested from any one class, provided that some of the class feel a name is appropriate.

During the week add more leaves as further evidence is found. If hundreds of pieces of evidence are offered, make the tree larger! The tree could be left up for some weeks, particularly if it is used during Lent or Advent.

This reading is about the true meaning of love—the way that Jesus loved his disciples—and is taken from one of the most famous chapters in St John's Gospel, when Jesus is about to leave his disciples. John 13.33–35:

'My children, I shall not be with you very much longer. You will look for me; but I tell you now what I told the Jewish authorities, "You cannot go where I am going." And now I give you a new commandment: love one another. As I have loved you, so you must love one another. If you have love for one another, then everyone will know that you are my disciples.'

(For school assembly.)
'I may speak in the tongues' (*BBC Complete Come and Praise* 100)

Arrange a focal point (or more if needed). This could be a picture to represent love, for example a mother and baby, or animal and baby, or a kitten or puppy.

Ask pupils to focus on the picture or to close their eyes, whichever they prefer. Then ask them to imagine the following. (Allow a moment or two between each of the suggestions!)

- Being touched by someone who loves you, for example when you have had a fall.

- Your room is in a terrible mess, but someone offers to come and help you clear it up.

- The first day at a new school and someone is very nice to you.

Close each scene with: 'Lord God, help us to love others as we love ourselves.' Then use the following prayer, if desired, to close this session.

Lord God,
You have shown us the real meaning of love
   by giving us your Son,
   Jesus Christ to teach us.
Help us to follow his example
   and to love other people
   in the same way that we love ourselves.   Amen.

➡ *RE*

Follow up the assembly idea by looking at the meaning of Good Friday and Easter. Alternatively, try imagining 'love' as any of the following: love as an animal; love as a toy; love as a flower; love as a person.

Art
Select from the images used above and create collage work. Review the work, and display under the title 'Love is . . .'.

English
Read *The Velveteen Rabbit* by Marjorie Williams and talk about loving someone or something.

History
As part of the study unit Britain since 1930 collect evidence from the local community of heroism during peace or war time (medals, eye-witness reports, newspaper cuttings etc.).

Kindness (school or class assembly)

Showing kindness to other people is another piece of evidence that we are keeping Jesus' commandment to love one another.

Create a board game on an over-head projector or board. On the left side of the screen, in a vertical position, have four or five pictures of children. These could be drawn in stick fashion, or as round heads with smiles.

The aim is to move each child across the 'page' to the far right. There should be two signposts, one saying 'This way!' and another saying 'Kindness', in bold letters. Both should point to the right.

Explain that the idea is to answer the questions and to try and move the figure across the board. *Do not talk about kindness at this stage.* Have to hand a number of questions to ask pupils. When the questions are answered you may wish to consult the whole school as to the answer, or else decide the correct answer yourself.

When the answers are correct (i.e., 'kind') the figure on the board advances (draw the figure further along the path) towards the right-hand side of the page. When the answers are unkind the figure meanders backwards.

QUESTIONS

- Mary has some sweets. Should she share them with Robert?
- James has borrowed his brother's bike and punctured the tyre. Should he tell him?
- Hazel hates Mary. Teacher thinks Mary has been talking in class, but really it was Hazel. What should Mary do?
- Jennie has a cat which often scratches her. What should Jennie do when this happens?
- David is going to play football with his friends and sees his grandmother. What should he do—go and play football or stay and help his grandmother carry her shopping?
- Gill has a new computer game. Sally comes to stay, but she does not know how to play computer games, and this one would be difficult for her anyway. What should Gill do?
- Ben has saved up £10 for a new football. He breaks a window, but no one knows that he has done it; in fact his parents think Darren's broken it and Darren's in dead trouble. If Ben tells his parents that it was his fault they will take his savings to repair the window. What should he do?
- It is Sarah's first day at school and she is very unhappy. Clare has been at school for six months and has many friends. She thinks Sarah is rather silly, and anyway she wants to tell all her friends about her holiday abroad. What should Clare do?
- Darryl has a new bike. A cousin comes to stay, who does not have a bike. Should Darryl stay and play with his cousin or go out on his bike for a ride with his friends?
- There are three cakes left on the plate and four people around your table. What should you do?

This week we are looking for evidence that we are following Jesus' instructions to live a new kind of life—the kind of life that God wants us to live. One of the pieces of evidence that tells us we are on the right track and doing what God wants is if we show kindness to one another.

In the game we have just played, the only way we managed to move the figure along the board was if we made a kind answer. When we were unkind the figure moved backwards! It is not always easy to know what we should do, but if we ask ourselves the question 'Are we being kind?' it might help us to know what to do.

◆ One of the kindest actions mentioned in the Bible is about a young woman who was prepared to leave her own home to travel with her mother-in-law to a strange land to keep her company. Ruth 1.1–11a, 14–17:

Long ago, in the days before Israel had a king, there was a famine in the land. So a man named Elimelech, who belonged to the clan of Ephrath and who lived in Bethlehem in Judah, went with his wife Naomi and their two sons Mahlon and Chilion to live for a while in the country of Moab. While they were living there, Elimelech died, and Naomi was left alone with her two sons, who married Moabite girls, Orpah and Ruth. About ten years later Mahlon and Chilion also died, and Naomi was left all alone, without husband or sons.

Some time later Naomi heard that the Lord had blessed his people by giving them a good harvest; so she got ready to leave Moab with her daughters-in-law. They started out together to go back to Judah, but on the way she said to them, 'Go back home and stay with your mothers. May the Lord be as good to you as you have been to me and to those who have died. And may the Lord make it possible for each of you to marry again and have a home.'

So Naomi kissed them good-bye. But they started crying and said to her, 'No! We will go with you to your people.'

'You must go back, my daughters,' Naomi answered . . . Again they started crying. Then Orpah kissed her mother-in-law goodbye and went back home, but Ruth held on to her. So Naomi said to her, 'Ruth, your sister-in-law has gone back to her people and to her god. Go back home with her.'

But Ruth answered, 'Don't ask me to leave you! Let me go with you. Wherever you go, I will go; wherever you live, I will live. Your people will be my people, and your God will be my God. Wherever you die, I will die, and that is where I will be buried. May the Lord's worst punishment come upon me if I let anything but death separate me from you!'

♫ (For school assembly.)
'Lead me from death to life' (*BBC Complete Come and Praise* 140)

✋ Lord God,
When Jesus lived on earth he was kind to people.
Help us to be kind to those around us,
    to think of other people before ourselves,
      and to try and put ourselves in their shoes.   Amen.

Note: Add more leaves to the tree, as described in the previous assembly, if pupils or teachers show evidence of love or kindness.

➡️ RE
Discuss some of the questions that came up in the game played during the assembly, and talk about various solutions to the problems.

History
As part of Britain since 1930, explore the war-time spirit of neighbourliness and ask older members of the community for their help.

English
Read *The BFG* by Roald Dahl.

Joy (school or class assembly)

The third piece of evidence that shows we are living the life that God requires of us is joy. This assembly explores the meaning of the word joy today.

Brainstorm the word 'Joy'. For example:

Joy is laughing for no reason.   Joy is a name.
Joy is giggling with a friend.   Joy is running across a field.

If pupils do not know what the word means, look at its dictionary definition: 'intense (or great) gladness'. Perhaps 'being *very* happy' might suffice.

Encourage pupils to think about those times in their lives when something sends a shiver through them—perhaps something beautiful (someone singing, or a picture?)—or times when they have cried out of sheer happiness.

Joy is another piece of evidence that tells us we are becoming the kind of person God wants us to become. Joy is that time when we feel as though the world is wonderful—as though we want to shout and sing, or to smile all the time.

We cannot feel happy and joyful all the time, but neither should we spend time moaning and grumbling about things that are not important. We should all try to be more joyful—but without pretending. Most of us have much to be happy about—we are alive, we have food, we have clothes, we are loved. (This needs saying even if there are children from homes where no one seems to love them, since God loves them!)

Today's story is about someone who was happy because she and her family and friends had been saved by God from drowning or from being killed by the Egyptian soldiers. We are told she danced for joy. Exodus 14.21–22; 15.19–21:

Moses held out his hand over the sea, and the Lord drove the sea back with a strong east wind. It blew all night and turned the sea into dry land. The water was divided, and the Israelites went through the sea on dry ground, with walls of water on both sides . . .

The Israelites walked through the sea on dry ground. But when the Egyptian chariots with their horses and drivers went into the sea, the Lord brought the water back, and it covered them.

The prophet Miriam, Aaron's sister, took her tambourine, and all the women followed her, playing tambourines and dancing. Miriam sang for them:

'Sing to the Lord, because he has won a glorious victory;
he has thrown the horses and their riders into the sea.'

Encourage pupils to hold hands in a huge circle (up and down the rows if there are a large number of pupils) and to raise their arms on the words 'joyful' and 'joy'.

Lord God,
Help us to remember to be joyful.   (*raise arms*)
You have given us so many things to make us happy,
    but often we forget to be joyful.   (*raise arms*)
Help us not to waste time grumbling about life.
And give us the gift of quiet joy.   (*raise arms*)
Amen.

(For school assembly)
'You shall go out with joy' (*BBC Complete Come and Praise* 98)
This song could be sung as the pupils lead out of the room, and repeated until everyone has left.

Note: Add more leaves to the tree if there has been evidence of joy, love or kindness by teachers or pupils.

> ➡️ *PE*
> Look at joy in PE by creating a joyful dance on the lines of a traditional Hebrew circle dance.
>
> *Music*
> Listen to a joyful piece of music, for example the Cachucha from Act 2 of *The Gondoliers* by Gilbert and Sullivan.
>
> *English*
> Learn the words of Psalm 100 or 150 using a modern version of the Bible. Discuss the meaning of joy in different contexts, e.g., in worship, at a football match, on getting a new puppy or kitten etc.
>
> *RE*
> Study the Beatitudes (Matthew 5.1–12), using the Good News version of the Bible which has 'Happy are they . . .'.

Patience (class assembly)

Patience is the fourth piece of evidence that our lives are on the right track and that we are living the sort of life that God desires.

Another piece of evidence that shows we are living the kind of life that God wants us to live is that we have patience. Some of us have more natural patience than others, just as some of us are kinder or more joyful. However, there should still be signs of patience in all of us.

When we are patient, we can wait; for instance we can wait in a queue. When we are patient, we can do things over and over again: we can practise scoring a goal, or getting a rounder, or making a tower of cards, even though we have to try it over and over again until we achieve our aim.

 Use a pack of children's 'Snap' cards to make a house of cards—or as much of a 'house' as is possible.

Ensure that the cards fall down a few times. Each time start again, with great patience. Allow pupils to try if suitable.

Jesus knew a lot about patience. After two or three years with his disciples Jesus sees, in this story, that they have learnt very little. Luke 9.37–42:

> The next day Jesus and the three disciples went down from the hill, and a large crowd met Jesus. A man shouted from the crowd. 'Teacher I beg you, look at my son—my only son! A spirit attacks him with a sudden shout and throws him into a fit, so that he foams at the mouth; it keeps on hurting him and will hardly let him go! I begged your disciples to drive it out, but they couldn't.'
>
> Jesus answered, 'How unbelieving and wrong you people are! How long must I stay with you?' Then he said to the man, 'Bring your son here.'
>
> As the boy was coming, the demon knocked him to the ground and threw him into a fit. Jesus gave a command to the evil spirit, healed the boy, and gave him back to his father. All the people were amazed at the mighty power of God.

Lord God,
Teach us to have patience with each other:
    to listen to one another,
    and to learn from one another.
  Help us to be patient with ourselves
    and also with you.   Amen.

Note: Add more leaves to the tree as desired to cover love, kindness, joy and patience.

Art
Follow up the assembly by doing some artwork requiring great patience: for example, create a collage by applying glue to a photocopy of an intricate picture then cover with sand, pasta, or straw to create a 3-D effect.

RE
Read the story of Jesus in the Garden: Mark 14:32–42, where Jesus shows remarkable patience. Talk about how Jesus must have felt let down by his friends. How might they have felt?

English
Read the chapter from *What Katy Did* by Susan Coolidge headed 'Dismal Days' which describes Katy's life in bed after she has fallen out of the swing. Write letters from a godmother to a godchild explaining why it is important to be patient.

Faithfulness (school or class assembly)

Faithfulness is the fifth piece of evidence that we might find in someone who is living the life that God wants us to live.

Encourage one or two teachers and pupils to bring their most favourite teddies to the assembly—preferably those owned since babyhood that still have pride of place in their home.

Ask the volunteers to talk about their teddy. When were they given it, and what did it look like when they first had it?

Discuss other toys that they subsequently received, and which may have taken their attention away from the original toy (a bike, a doll, skates etc.). Elicit from them that although new toys came along, their favourite teddy was always there to come back to at the end of the day, and is still with them today even though other toys have come and gone.

Another piece of evidence to show that we are living the kind of life God wants us to lead is faithfulness.

Faithfulness is about staying with someone or something. For instance, if we have a friend it means we do not go off to play with someone else, leaving our friend alone. If we have a job to do, we are faithful when we keep on going until the job is finished. So, for instance, Christians keep faithful to God no matter how difficult things get.

In Bunyan's book *Pilgrim's Progress*, Faithful is Christian's friend. Faithful follows Christian wherever he goes, until finally he is killed in the city of Vanity.

Another person who showed great faithfulness is St Paul, one of Jesus' earliest followers. He was hounded from city to city by other Jews who disliked this new Christian who as a Pharisee had once been on their side. Often they beat him and threw him into prison, yet even here he remains faithful. Acts 16.16–31:

One day as we were going to the place of prayer, we were met by a slave-girl who had an evil spirit that enabled her to predict the future. She earned a lot of money for her owners by telling fortunes. She followed Paul and us, shouting, 'These men are servants of the Most High God! They announce to you how you can be saved!' She did this for many days, until Paul became so upset that he turned round and said to the spirit, 'In the name of Jesus Christ I order you to come out of her!' The spirit went out of her that very moment.

When her owners realized that their chance of making money was gone, they seized Paul and Silas and dragged them to the authorities in the public square. They brought them before the Roman officials and said, 'These men are Jews, and they are causing trouble in our city. They are teaching customs that are against our law; we are Roman citizens, and we cannot accept these customs or practise them.' And the crowd joined in the attack against Paul and Silas.

Then the officials tore the clothes off Paul and Silas and ordered them to be whipped. After a severe beating, they were thrown into jail, and the jailer was ordered to lock them up tight. Upon receiving this order, the jailer threw them into the inner cell and fastened their feet between heavy blocks of wood.

About midnight Paul and Silas were praying and singing hymns to God, and the other prisoners were listening to them. Suddenly there was a violent earthquake, which shook the prison to its foundations. At once all the doors opened, and the chains fell off all the prisoners. The jailer woke up, and when he saw the prison doors open, he thought that the prisoners had escaped; so he pulled out his sword and was about to kill himself. But Paul shouted at the top of his voice, 'Don't harm yourself! We are all here!'

The jailer called for a light, rushed in, and fell trembling at the feet of

Paul and Silas. Then he led them out and asked, 'Sirs, what must I do to be saved?'

They answered, 'Believe in the Lord Jesus, and you will be saved—you and your family.'

 'O Lord, all the world' (*BBC Complete Come and Praise* 39)

 Lord God,
Very often we are not faithful to our friends or family,
   and often we are not faithful to you
Teach us what faithfulness means,
      so that one day we may know that we have been your faithful
      subjects throughout our lives.   Amen.

RE
Follow up the idea of faithfulness by finding out about a Celtic saint, like Cuthbert. He lived as a hermit on the Farne Islands off the Northumbrian coast. Try to work out what his life might have been like in such a place. Talk about being faithful to God under these circumstances.

History
As part of one of the study units, make a study of someone who is killed for 'wrong thinking' (e.g., Aristotle).

Art
Following all the pieces of evidence in the last five assemblies, look at the words from Galatians 5.22–23 about the fruits of the Spirit, and create collage work using these words.

Useful Addresses

World development

Christian Aid
PO Box 100
London
SE1 7RT

Catholic Fund for Overseas Development (CAFOD)
2 Romero Close
London
SW9 9TY

One World Week
PO Box 100
London
SE1 7RT

Oxfam
274 Banbury Road
Oxford
OX2 7DZ

Save the Children
Education Unit
17 Grove Lane
London
SE5 8RD

Tear Fund
100 Church Road
Teddington
Middlesex
TW11 8QE

UNICEF
25 Churchgater
Leicester
LE1 3AL

World Development Movement (WDM)
25 Beehive Place
London
SW9 7QR

Church overseas

Church Missionary Society (CMS)
157 Waterloo Road
London
SE1 8UU

Leprosy Mission
Goldhay Way
Orton Goldhay
Peterborough
PE2 5GZ

Society for Promoting Christian Knowledge (SPCK)
Holy Trinity Church
Marylebone Road
London
NW1 4DU

United Society for the Propagation of the Gospel (USPG)
157 Waterloo Road
London
SE1 8XA

Environment

Friends of the Earth (FOE)
26 Underwood Street
London
N1 7JQ

Greenpeace
Canonbury Villas
London
N1 2PN

Prisoners of conscience

Amnesty International
99 Roseberry Avenue
London
EC1 4RE

Race

Campaign for Racial Equality
Elliott House
Allington Street
London
SW1E 7EH

Poverty

Child Poverty Action Group
1 Bath Street
London
EC1V 9DX

Christian Action
St Anselm's Church Hall
Kennington Cross
Kennington Road
London
SE11 5DU

Families

Exploring Parenthood
Latimer Education Centre
194 Freston Road
London
W10 6TT

National Council for One Parent Families
255 Kentish Town Road
London
NW5 2LX

Gingerbread
35 Wellington Street
London
WC2E 7BN

Stepfamily
72 Willesden Lane
London
NW6 7TA

Family Life and Marriage Education (FLAME)
11 Mundy Street
Heanor
Derbyshire
DE7 7EB

Book List

Hymn books

BBC Complete Come and Praise (BBC 1990).
Mission Praise (Marshall Pickering, 1990).
Junior Praise (Marshall Pickering, 1986).

Other books referred to

Elaine Brown, *The Surprise Present* (Lion 1979).
Roald Dahl, *The BFG* (Cape 1982).
Taffy Davies, *Miles and the Computer* (Scripture Union 1987).
Meryl Doney, *The Very Worried Sparrow* (Lion 1991).
Angela Elwell, *The Tale of Three Trees* (Lion 1989).
Toni Goffe, *Bully for You* (Child's Play 1991).
Ted Hughes, *The Iron Woman* (Faber and Faber 1993).
Shirley Hughes, *Giving* (Walker Books 1993).
Ezra Jack Keats, *Peter's Chair* (Bodley Head 1968).
The Lord's Prayer for Children Retold (Lion 1993).
Grace Nichols (ed.), *Can I Buy a Slice of the Sky?* (Penguin/Blackie 1992).
Oxfam 50 (Collins and Brown 1992).
W. Ellwood Post, *Saints, Signs and Symbols* (SPCK 1975).
Brian Sibley, *The Frightful Food Feud* (Lion 1994).
Jill Tomlinson, *The Owl who was Afraid of the Dark* (Macmillan 1988).
Brian Wildsmith, *The True Cross* (Oxford University Press 1987).
David Wilkerson, *The Cross and the Switchblade* (Lakeland Publishing 1964).
Marjorie Williams, *The Velveteen Rabbit* (Heinemann, 1983).